Contents

To the student   1

1   **Sleeping habits**   3

2   **Good buys**   6

3   **Know yourself**   10

4   **Flat hunting**   15

5   **Getting there**   20

6   **Missing plans**   23

7   **Great expectations**   27

8   **One-upmanship**   32

9   **Exit 13**   37

10   **Left out?**   42

11   **Football crazy, football mad**   47

Transcripts   51

Key to exercises   84

To the teacher   101
Principles   101
What the units contain   103
Suggestions for teaching procedure   104

Acknowledgements

The authors wish to thank Françoise Grellet who provided the photographs used in the book and also the staff of the Pilgrim's Language Courses at the University of Kent (Summer 1980) for their helpful criticism and valuable suggestions.

The A.A. advised route on page 37 is reprinted by permission of The Automobile Association; the photograph on page 42 is reproduced by permission of Leo Burnett Ltd, Advertising.

A.M.
S.M.

To the student

Learning to Listen is designed to help you improve your understanding of spoken English. The book and recordings can be used most profitably with the help of a teacher and fellow students, but the provision of an answer key and transcripts make it possible for you to study on your own.

Its objective is to show you:

1 how to use the English you already have.
2 how you can gradually build upon what you know.
3 how you can prove for yourself that your understanding of spoken English is increasing.

Learning to Listen does this by presenting the material to you in easy steps.

PRE-LISTENING

Before listening to each recording, you will have the opportunity of either looking at a picture, reading an advertisement, for example, or simply discussing the topic. This will help you familiarize yourself with the theme of the unit and certain necessary vocabulary.

LISTENING

Your teacher will then play the recording for you as many times as you wish. In this way, you can listen without feeling rushed. Your main objective at this stage is just to get the main ideas of the topic.

INTENSIVE LISTENING

In this step, you will be asked to listen for certain specific information. But, once again, help will be provided. You will find a grid in which you have to write the information. Time will be given for you to study this grid carefully first. In the earlier units of the book, some of the information may already be given to help guide you in your listening.

In some units, your attention will be focussed on particular language features, for example, the way things are said or the manner in which they are said, or the intonation of the speakers. Exercises on these features will help you understand the full meaning of the spoken message.

CHECKING UP

You will always be able to read the transcript at the end of each unit as there will probably be things which still puzzle you. Do try, however, to piece together as much as possible of the information you have with the help of your teacher and fellow students. Do *not* underestimate what you think you have understood.

RELATED ACTIVITIES

Most of the units contain some different activities linked to the topic of the unit. You can use these to see how much of the information and language you have understood and can use yourself in similar situations to those in the units.

SOME POINTS TO REMEMBER

1 *Learning to Listen* aims *to help* you understand, *not to test* your understanding.
2 You may leave out certain activities and come back to them later if you find them difficult.
3 You will always be able to understand *something*. It is by building on this 'something' that you will come to understand more.

Some exercises have a key symbol (🗝) beside them. This means that the answer to the exercise is given at the back of the book.

Unit 1 Sleeping habits

Pre-listening

1 a) Look carefully at this questionnaire.

What are your sleeping habits?

A short questionnaire
to discover your
sleeping habits

1 How much time do you
   spend on bedmaking?
   a) 5 mins a day
   b) 5 mins every other day
   c) 5 mins a week

2 Before you go to bed do you
   a) pull open the downstairs
      curtains
   b) read
   c) eat

3 After a night's sleep do you
   find that the covers
   a) are as tidy as when you went
      to bed
   b) are all over the floor
   c) are in a heap in the middle of
      the bed

4 If you have trouble getting to
   sleep do you
   a) count sheep
   b) toss and turn
   c) lie still and concentrate

5 If you wake up in the middle
   of the night is it because
   a) you remember something
      you ought to have done
   b) you're cold
   c) you're hungry

6 If you hear a bump in the
   night do you
   a) get up cautiously and
      investigate quietly
   b) charge around the house
      with a weapon
   c) turn over and go back to sleep

7 Do other people complain
   about your sleeping habits?
   a) never
   b) frequently
   c) sometimes

8 When you have dreams are
   they mostly
   a) dreams about work
   b) nightmares
   c) sweet dreams

Make sure that you understand all the words in it and that
you know how they are pronounced.

b) Now, working in pairs, one of you should interview the
other using this questionnaire. If there is time, change roles
(that is, the interviewer should now be interviewed).

3

Listening

2 a) You will now hear a recorded interview on the tape. You should work on your own. As you listen, note down which of the suggested answers is nearest to the one given on the tape. If none of them fit, then try to note down what the answer was. Do not worry if you do not get all the information the first time. You will hear the tape at least three times. 🗝

   b) When you have finished, work with a partner and compare your answers. Then check your answers with the teacher.

3 a) Stay with the same partner. You will now hear a second version of the interview. This time the interviewer does not ask all the questions and they are not in the same order as in the printed questionnaire. Once again try to decide which of the printed answers is nearest to the one given on the tape. 🗝

   b) When you have finished, compare your answers in groups of four. Then check them with the teacher.

Intensive listening

4 a) Listen carefully to the first interview again, in pairs. This time try to find which of the man's sentences match the following reported sentences.
   e.g. He explained that he had very little time.
         'Well I'm in a bit of a hurry.'

   i)   He expressed concern that the interviewer might be invading his privacy.
   ii)   His opinion was that bedmaking was women's work.
   iii) He had been told that he did not move much in his sleep.
   iv)   He answered that generally he had no problems in getting to sleep.
   v)   He disagreed that he was courageous – simply annoyed.
   vi)   He denied that other people had complained.
   vii) He explained that he almost always forgot his dreams.
   Check your answers with those of another pair. 🗝

4 b) Now do the same thing using interview 2.
- i) He expressed reservations about the type of questions.
- ii) He explained that he rarely had any difficulty in falling asleep.
- iii) He explained that reading sent him to sleep.
- iv) He found his dreams somewhat disturbing.
- v) He denied that he snored.
- vi) He agreed that he occupied more than half of the bed.
- vii) He dismissed any complaints that people made. ⚏

Checking up

5 a) Listen to interview 1 again in groups of four. As you listen, note down in your own way (don't worry about the spelling) any words or phrases which you still do not understand. When you have finished, compare your notes with the others in the group. Perhaps someone else can help explain what you did not understand, and you may be able to help others. Finally, check any remaining problems by reading through the transcript on pages 51–5.

b) If there is time, work through interview 2 in the same way.

Unit 2 Good buys

Pre-listening

1 First of all, read this shopping list. Make sure that you know
  what each of the items is and how it is pronounced.

Shopping list

1 Chicken (not frozen)
1 lb Guernsey tomatoes
¼ lb mushrooms
2 Spanish onions
1 lb long grain rice
1 crisp lettuce
1 bottle of olive oil
1 bottle of wine vinegar
½ lb Gorgonzola cheese
French bread
1 carton of cream
strawberries

Listening

2 This list was made by a woman for her husband who has just
  returned with the shopping. You will now hear the man and
  his wife discussing the goods as he unpacks them.
  Unfortunately he did not get exactly what was on the list.

As you listen, note down in the grid below:
i) what he bought correctly.
ii) what things he bought instead.
iii) what he must return to the shop for.

Correct purchases	Alternatives purchased	Goods to return and buy

You will hear the recording three times, so do not worry if you do not get all the information the first time.

3 Now discuss your answers with the person sitting next to you.
As you talk try to include sentences like:
He bought . . . instead of . . .
Instead of buying . . . he bought . . .
He should've bought . . . not . . .
When you have finished discuss your answers with the teacher.

Intensive listening

4 We hear sometimes that the man is not certain about whether his purchases are correct, so he quickly adds an excuse or explanation as to why he did not buy exactly what was needed. Listen to the tape again and note down *in your own words* either the item or the excuse.

	Goods	Excuses
i)	Single cream	
ii)		'Just a few because they were a bit expensive.'
iii)	Pickling onions	

	Goods	Excuses
iv)		'No they won't. They're very firm.'
v)		'It has got a bit squashed, I'm sorry about that.'
vi)	Vegetable oil	
vii)	Rice	

Recognizing and interpreting attitudes

5 This time, listen to the woman's remarks about each item. Can
you recognize and interpret her attitude from the words and
tone she uses. Listen to the tape and identify the remarks in the
grid below. Write next to the remark the number which
corresponds to the attitude taken by the woman. You may
consider that her remark can be interpreted by more than one
of the attitudes listed below. If so, note down the other
numbers and, after listening, discuss your selection with your
partner and teacher.

Attitudes:
Sarcasm 1   Reluctant acceptance 2   Acceptance with
understanding 3   Objection 4   Patience 5
Irritation 6

	Goods	Remarks	Attitude number
i)	Cream	'Ooh dear! Well I, well I suppose yes I can beat it up ...'	
ii)	Strawberries	'Well, all right. O.K.'	
iii)	Chicken	'Well, I suppose if it was the best you could get, it was the best you could get.'	
iv)	Tomatoes	'Well thank you for putting them under the chicken.'	
v)	Onions	'No dear! They're pickling onions.'	
vi)	Rice	'Yes dear, I wanted long grain rice.'	

	Goods	Remarks	Attitude number
vii)	Lettuce	'I asked you to get me a crisp lettuce.'	
viii)	Oil	'Oh, darling, no.'	
ix)	Herbs	'Well you'd better put that on your list with the onions.'	
x)	Cheese	'You've not left it on the counter, have you?'	

Checking up

6 Listen to the tape again in groups of four. As you listen, note down in your own way (don't worry about the spelling) any words and phrases which you still do not understand. When you have finished, compare notes with the others in your group. Perhaps someone else can help explain what you did not understand, and you may be able to help others. Finally, check any remaining problems by reading through the transcript on pages 55–7.

Group work

7 Divide into groups of five. Each group should compile a shopping list of items to buy (not necessarily food). When this has been done, each group sends a member to the next group with the list. He does not show the list, but merely reads it aloud once. Meanwhile the group members may take notes. Now each group sends one of its members to the next group with the list it has just received. Again it is read aloud and notes taken. The same procedure is followed until the list comes back to the original group.
  Notice any changes?

Unit 3   Know yourself

Pre-listening

1   First of all, look carefully at the chart below. Make sure that
    you know what all the words mean and how they are
    pronounced.

	Outstanding	Above average	Average	Below average	Poor
Loving					
Selfish					
Sexy					
Loyal					
Jealous					
Secretive					

Listening

2   This chart appeared in a magazine. You will now hear a
    woman filling it in with help from her husband. She keeps
    trying to get his agreement to the score she wishes to give
    herself. Eventually they come to agreement about each of her
    qualities. As you listen, put a tick in the box which corresponds
    to their agreed decision for each quality. You will hear the
    recording three times, so do not worry if you do not get all the
    information the first time. ⚷

3 Now discuss your answers with the person sitting next to you.
You may find it helpful to begin some of your sentences in
some of these ways:
I'm sure . . .
I'm not quite sure but I think . . .
I thought they . . .
It wasn't very clear but it seemed that . . .
When you have finished discuss your decisions with the teacher
and the rest of the class.

4 Work in pairs to discuss who you think the two people are and
what they are like (their age, their jobs, their characters etc.)
Now look at the six pictures below and decide which two of
these people were talking to each other. Compare your
decision with another pair.

Intensive listening 1

5 Each of the two speaker tries to justify his/her opinion by
referring to *past events* or *experience*. For each of the qualities
note down the arguments used in the grid below. (In some
cases there are none, in others more than one.)

	Woman's arguments	*Man's arguments*
Loving	I've put up with you for the past ten years.	
Selfish		
Sexy		
Loyal		
Jealous		
Secretive		

Discuss your results with your partner, then with the teacher
and the rest of the class.

Intensive listening 2

6 a) The couple disagree with each other about a lot of things.
For example, they say:
'Well, I wouldn't say that . . .'
'No, no . . .'
Rubbish . . .'
Listen to the tape again. This time ask the teacher to stop the
tape every time you hear the couple disagree. Try to write
down the phrase or sentence they use. At the end divide into
groups of four and see how many different ways of
disagreeing you have in each group. ⚷

   b) Many of the sentences the couple use begin,
'What about . . .'
But these sentences do not always mean the same thing. The
person may be:
i)   requesting further information.
ii)   making an accusation.
iii) asking someone's opinion.
iv)   giving an example.
v)   making an objection.
Listen to the tape again. Ask the teacher to stop it each time you
come to a sentence beginning 'What about'. Discuss which of the
above meanings the sentence has. ⚷

Checking up

7 Listen to the tape again in groups of four. As you listen, note
down in your own way (don't worry about the spelling) any
words or phrases you still do not understand. When you have
finished, compare notes with the others in your group. Perhaps
someone else can help to explain what you did not understand,
and you may be able to help him. Finally, check any remaining
problems by reading through the transcript on pages 57–60.

Group work

8 a) Look at the chart below:

	Outstanding	Above average	Average	Below average	Poor
Loving	5	4	3	2	1
Selfish	1	2	3	4	5
Sexy	5	4	3	2	1
Loyal	5	4	3	2	1
Jealous	1	2	3	4	5
Secretive	1	2	3	4	5

The numbers in each box are the scores for the different qualities.

Now draw an empty grid on a sheet of paper. Think carefully about yourself and place ticks in the corresponding boxes. (If you do not wish to answer any of the questions leave that column blank.) Then count up the points you have scored.

Key: If you have 30 you are a saint!
If you have 20 or more you are nicer than most people.
If you have 15 you are O.K., but only just!
If you have less than 15 – try changing some of your habits!

b) Now work in groups of four. See if the other three members of the group agree with the way you have scored yourself. If not, why not?

Unit 4 Flat hunting

Pre-listening

1 Scan these advertisements in pairs and with the help of your
partner (the teacher if necessary) decide what the abbreviations
mean. Make a note of them, as you will need them for
exercise 3.

CHELSEA. Immac 1st fl. flat. 1 b, sit-rm,
new k&b, gar. £70 p.w. Tel: 374 4638
(2-5 only)
CHELSEA. Flood St. Eleg 1st fl. maisonette
in PB bl. access to gdn. 1 dbl. b, b,
recep., fitted k, c.h. £100 p.w. Tel: 374
4827
TITE ST, CHELSEA. Immac 2nd fl. flat.
Prize loc. lge recep., 1 b, newly fitted
k&b, gar., no pets, £95 p.w. Tel: 374
9260
WEST KEN. Spac. fam. flat in mansion bl.
2 recep., 4 bed., lge k&b, diner, balc.,
gar. Sunny, £200 p.w. Tel: 734 1617
SOUTH KEN. Quiet flat in prestige bl.
Use of lge gdn. 2 bed., lge recep., din.,
hall, b, shower, mod. k, £125 p.w. Tel:
734 8210
KENSINGTON. Gdn flt. w. lge recep. 2 b,
bath, new country style k, no pets, gar.
£120 p.w. Tel: 734 6355
MAYFAIR W1. Delightful quiet 1st fl. flat
in exc. order. Pretty sun terr. Tel: 234
1212 (after 6p.m. only)
CLOSE OXFORD ST. 4 rm. flt., 3 bed., 2 b,
w.c., lounge, k, £160 p.w. Tel: 620 4690
ST. JAMES, GREEN PARK. Mod bl., 4th
fl. flat. 3 bed., 2 b, w.c., 2 rec., unfurn.,
oil c.h. £200 p.w. Tel: 499 9981
PIMLICO. Exc. 3 bed., conv. bl., close to
tube, buses, shops, lge recep., open fire-
place, k&b, gas c.h. Tel: 923 6575

Note down some of the abbreviations and their meanings here.
Example: b. – bathroom or bedroom. 🗝

Listening

2 Your teacher is now going to play a recording for you. First,
read through the following points in preparation and, after

15

listening to the conversation, jot down the answers in the space provided.

i)   What is the topic of the conversation?   ....

ii) How many speakers are involved in the conversation?   ....

iii) How would you describe the attitudes of the the different speakers?   ....

iv) What do you think accounts for these attitudes?   ....

Discuss your replies with your partner. ⚷

3 In this exercise, you will hear the same recording again. This time, however, listen for details of the flats. Using the grid below as a guide, note down the location of the flat in column 1, and as many details as you can in column 2. Some of the locations have been given to you. Remember, you will not be able to write down everything the first time, so your teacher will play the recording again. However, if you use the abbreviations discussed in exercise 1, this will enable you to work more quickly.

	Location	Details of flats
i)		
ii)		
iii)		
iv)	The Angel	
v)		
vi)	Hampstead	
vii)		

Check these details with a friend first before turning to the map on page 19 where you will find the missing details. ⚷

Intensive listening

4 a) First read the expression listed below and then listen again for the actual expressions used by John with regard to the flats and which are similar in meaning to those given. When you think you have discovered them, jot them down in the space provided.

	Discussion point	*Meaning*	*Actual expression used*
i)	Chelsea	They are asking an extortionate price for it.	
ii)	Bayswater	I really don't want to spend more than . . .	
		I think that's expensive.	
iii)	The Angel	Well, I'll think about it.	
vi)	Hyde Park	Your advice is a great help, I don't think.	

🗝

b) Repeat this exercise, but this time listen for certain of the expressions used by Brenda.

	Discussion point	*Meaning*	*Actual expression used*
i)	Chelsea	Is that too expensive for you?	
ii)	Bayswater	I don't think you'll find anything cheaper.	
vi)	Hampstead	I don't think that's what they are thinking of.	
	Conclusion	I think you should try this one in Bayswater.	

🗝

Checking up

5 Listen to the tape again in groups of four. As you listen, note down in your own way (don't worry about the spelling) any words or phrases you still do not understand. When you have finished compare notes with the others in your group. Perhaps they can help you with your problems, and you may be able to help them. Finally, check any remaining problems by reading through the transcript on pages 60–2.

6 Read the descriptions of the flat hunters below. Look at the advertisements on the map of London and try to match up the flat hunters with the flats. When you have done this, compare your decisions with another student's. Make sure that you give reasons why you think a particular flat is more appropriate than another.

   i)   Three girls wish to share flat. Desire separate bedrooms. Central location required. Prepared to pay £50 p.w. ea.

   ii)   American family require lge flat/house. Have two children and dog. Require room for entertaining. Proximity to public services essential.

   iii)   Young couple need small flat, preferably with garden. Keep cats. Rent negotiable.

   iv)   Bachelor looking for 1 bedroom flat, preferably in Chelsea or West Ken. area. Garage essential.

   v)   Doctor and family require large flat/house. Three bed. min. Garage essential.

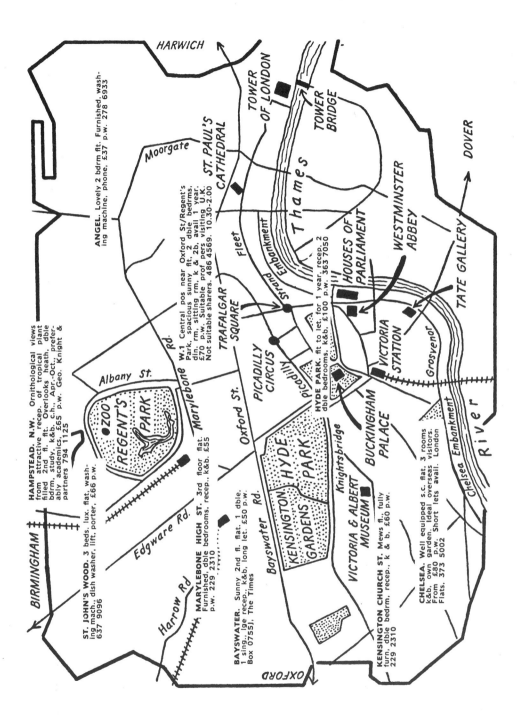

HARWICH

TOWER OF LONDON

TOWER BRIDGE

DOVER

ST. PAUL'S CATHEDRAL

Moorgate

ANGEL. Lovely 2 bdrm flt. Furnished, washing machine, phone. £37 p.w. 278 6933

Thames

Fleet

Strand Embankment

WESTMINSTER ABBEY

HOUSES OF PARLIAMENT

TATE GALLERY

W.1 Central pos near Oxford St/Regent's Park, spacious sunny flt, 2 dble bdrms, din. rm, sitting rm, k & 2b, avail 1 year. £70 p.w. Suitable prof pers visiting U.K. Not suitable sharers. 486 4569. 10.30-2.00

TRAFALGAR SQUARE

PICADILLY CIRCUS

Piccadilly

Marylebone Rd.

Oxford St.

Albany St.

ZOO

REGENT'S PARK

VICTORIA STATION

HYDE PARK. flt to let for 1 year, recep, 2 dble bedrooms. k&b. £100 p.w. 363 7050

Grosvenor

BUCKINGHAM PALACE

Knightsbridge

RIVER

Chelsea Embankment

BIRMINGHAM

Edgware Rd.

Harrow Rd.

ST. JOHN'S WOOD. 3 beds. lux. flat, washing mach, dish washer, lift, porter, £66 p.w. 637 9096

MARYLEBONE HIGH ST. 3rd floor flat. Furnished dble bedrooms, recep., k&b. £55 p.w. 229 2310

BAYSWATER. Sunny 2nd fl. flat. 1 dble. 1 sing., lge recep., k&b, long let. £50 p.w. Box 07551, The Times

Bayswater Rd.

HYDE PARK

KENSINGTON GARDENS

VICTORIA & ALBERT MUSEUM

KENSINGTON CHURCH ST. Mews fl. fully furn, dble bedrm, recep., k & b, £60 p.w. 229 2310

CHELSEA. Well equipped s.c. flat, 3 rooms k&b, own garden. Ideal overseas visitors. From £80 p.w. Short lets avail. London Flats. 373 5002

OXFORD

19

Pre-listening

1 a) First of all look at this advertisement.

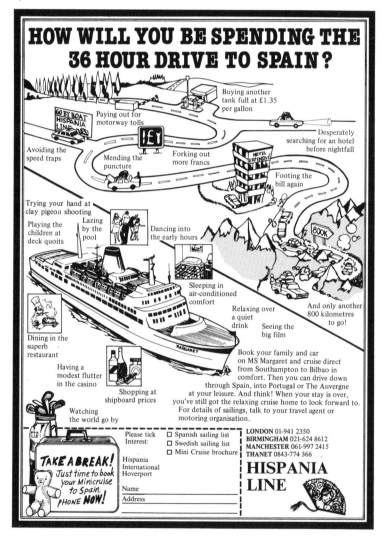

Make sure that you understand all the words in it and that you know how they are pronounced.

b) Now work with a partner and complete the following grid. Use the advertisement to make a list for columns 1 and 2. Make sure that you use all the information in the advertisement. Leave columns 3 and 4 blank for the moment.

Advantages of going by ship	√	*Disadvantages of going by car*	√	*Wife's objections*	*Advantages of going by car*

Listening

2 a) Now listen to the tape. You will hear a man and his wife discussing their holidays in Spain. He wants to go by ship and he uses some of the points mentioned in the advertisement. As you listen check off (√) on your grid the points 'for and against' which he actually mentions. Listen to the tape twice to make sure you have not missed any.

b) Now listen to the tape again. This time try with a partner to complete columns 3 and 4 by making a list of all the objections the wife makes and all the advantages she sees in going by car. You will probably need to listen to the recording several times.

c) Do you think the couple will go by ship or by car? Why?

Role-play

3 Work in pairs. Use the information in your grid to replay the scene. You can also use other arguments to persuade your partner – either those mentioned in the advertisement, or those you think of yourself.

Intensive listening

4 Listen to the tape again as far as the sentence 'I know you.' As you listen, try to find the spoken sentences which are similar in meaning to these written ones. When you hear one, stop the tape and write it down.

   e.g Why should we change our plans?
        'I don't see any reason to change our plans at all.'

   i)   He told me they enjoyed themselves a lot.
   ii)   That's not true.
   iii) I don't believe being on a boat is restful.
   iv)   What sort of things?
   v)   There may even be several films to choose from.
   vi)   Visiting historical buildings will take too long.
   vii) It was too expensive.
   viii) I prefer to pay for everything in advance.
   ix)   What other activities are there?
   x)   Going by boat must be very expensive. ⚿

Checking up

5 Listen to the tape again in groups of four. As you listen, note down in your own way any words or phrases you still do not understand. Then compare notes with the others in the group. Try to help each other resolve these difficulties. Finally, check any remaining problems by reading through the transcript on pages 62–4.

Unit 6 Missing plans

Pre-listening

1 Before you listen to the tape, read this newspaper article.

Rag trade rumpus

POLICE were called in this morning to investigate a break-in at the research laboratories of Wainwright Bros Ltd, Cheetham Hill, Manchester.

Thieves made off with top secret plans for a revolutionary new textile process.

Jeremy Wainwright, who was working on this new stain-proof process for children's fabrics on Saturday afternoon believes the theft took place between 6.30 p.m. when he left the laboratory and 10.15 p.m. when the night-watchman discovered the broken window.

Police are conducting enquiries among staff of the firm, and among members of the public who have recently visited the laboratories.

'This almost certainly is yet another case of industrial espionage,' Manchester Police Chief Watkins declared.

Listening

2 Now look at the grid below. You are going to hear recordings of some telephone calls made in the week preceding the theft. Some of these calls were made by staff at the textile plant or people who may have visited it recently. As you listen to the calls, note down the plans of each speaker (as in the example). Do not worry if you do not get all the information the first time. The tape will be played again.

Missing plans

	Monday	Tuesday	Wednesday	Thursday	Friday	Saturday	Sunday
1	←——In Bristol (lectures)——→						
2							
3							

3 Work in groups of three and compare the information each person has on his grid. With the teacher, all groups then contribute to filling in a master grid on the blackboard.

4 Now listen to the tape again. This time listen for these items of information only.
  i) The names of the people talking on the phone.
  ii) Their professions.
  iii) Their relationships to each other (good friends, colleagues, superior/inferior etc.)
  For (iii) try to find evidence for your opinion (e.g. in call 1 Bob says 'Hello my darling', which shows he is on very close terms with Anna).

Intensive listening

5 A list of adjectives follows, some of which might describe some of the characters in the phone calls. First of all, check that you know the meanings of the adjectives. Then listen to the tape again and try to match adjectives with characters. (Some characters may be described by more than one adjective and some adjectives may describe more than one character.) As you listen, jot down the phrases each character uses which support your choice of adjective. Then, work in pairs to exchange your ideas. Try to use sentences like these:
  If you want my opinion, Johnson is . . . because he says things like '. . .'
  For example, Johnson says things like '. . .' so he must be . . .

24

List of adjectives

respectful	placid	blunt
persuasive	business-like	eager
hesitant	self-important	disappointed
uncertain	enthusiastic	
anxious	authoritative	

Group work

6 The police decided to call Bob and Johnson for questioning. Johnson claims he stayed in Leeds on Saturday night and that his wife came up. Bob, the young textile designer and lecturer, also stayed in Leeds. They say they met in a pub on Saturday evening to discuss designs. Can they prove that they spent from 6.30 p.m. to 10.15 p.m. together?

  Two people should play the roles of Bob and Johnson. They should leave the room and work out in detail everything they did together between 6.30 p.m. and 10.15 p.m. on the Saturday

in question. (They must have been in at least three different places together.)

The rest of the class divides into two interrogation teams. While Bob and Johnson are out of the room the teams should prepare questions to ask them.

First Bob is called in and questioned by team 1. Any question is fair (e.g. How many people were in the pub? Was there a barman or a barmaid? Where were you sitting? etc.)

Then Johnson is questioned by team 2. If the teams manage to find three discrepancies between Bob's and Johnson's stories – they are guilty!

Checking up

7 Listen to the tape again in groups of four. As you listen, note down in your own way (don't worry about the spelling) any words or phrases which you still do not understand. When you have finished compare notes with the others in your group. Help each other to work out the difficulties. Finally, check any remaining problems by reading through the transcript on pages 64–7.

Unit 7   Great expectations

Pre-listening

1 a) Read this advertisement carefully.

```
┌─────────────────────────────────────┐
│                                       │
│       Junior Sales Manager            │
│   Expanding  pharmaceutical  export   │
│   firm seeks young junior sales mana- │
│   ger.  Excellent  prospects  for well-│
│   educated person with ambition and   │
│   drive.  Interesting and varied work │
│   including travel. Apply in writing to│
│   Personnel  Manager,  Pharmex  Ltd,  │
│   P.O. Box 222, Harlow New Town, Essex.│
│                                       │
└─────────────────────────────────────┘
```

Listening

b) Now listen to the first part of the recording. You will hear
the Personnel Manager of Pharmex Ltd talking to his secretary about the kind of person he wishes to recruit for the job
of junior sales manager. As you listen try to fill in the grid
below with the details of his 'ideal' candidate.

IDEAL QUALITIES

	What he wants	*What he does not want*
Sex		
Age		
Education		
Pay		

	What he wants	*What he does not want*
Attitude to overtime		
Accent/manner		
Other qualities		

Do not worry if you do not get all the information first time as you will hear the tape again. 🔑

2 Now that you know what the manager is looking for, work with a partner to prepare five questions you would want to ask any candidate if you were on the interviewing board. Compare your questions with those of another pair.

3 a) You will now hear three possible candidates for the job who have telephoned the manager for further details. As you listen, complete the grid below for each of them. How far do they fit the ideal qualities the manager requires?

	A	B	C
Sex			
Age			
Education			
Attitude to overtime			
Accent/manner			
Other qualities			

🔑

Discuss your notes in groups of three. Then try to decide which of the three you think would be most likely to get the job. Also discuss why the other two would not get it.

b) Look at the eight pictures below. Which three of them correspond to your idea of the candidates on the tape? Discuss your ideas in groups of three.

Intensive listening

4 Listen again to candidate A. Ths time stop the tape when you
come to each of these sentences:

'Well, I just thought it was right up my street you know.'

'I'm not really too worried about getting a large salary to start
with.'

'I do hope that my career as a secretary will lead me eventually
into management.'

'Oh, can't I arrange for an interview now?'

Which of the qualities below are revealed by these statements
(and the way they are spoken)?

enthusiasm	modesty	confusion
ambition	doubt	honesty
disappointment	confidence	lack of assurance
insensitivity		

Discuss your ideas with a partner. Now listen to candidates B
and C. Every time you hear a sentence which indicates one of
the above qualities, stop the tape and ask the teacher to write it
on the blackboard. Discuss the sentences as they come up. Does
everyone agree? 🗝

5 Here is an example of a reference for candidate A.

```
        TO WHOM IT MAY CONCERN

Miss Candida Fawcett is a highly competent and willing young lady.
She has worked with us here as a secretary for two years and has
always shown a high level of interest in her work.  Her abilities extend
far beyond the demands of a secretarial position and this is why we
are pleased she has applied for a more responsible job.  We feel that
with her drive and her excellent knowledge of French and Italian she
is an ideal candidate for the junior sales manager's post you are
advertising.  I have no hesitation in recommending her without reserve.

        Signed
```

In groups of three, write a reference for either candidate B or
C. Use the points you recorded in the grid as a guide. The reference for candidate B should be written by his ex-
headmaster, for candidate C by his previous employer. Discuss
your letter of reference with another group when you have
finished.

Checking up

6 Listen to the tape again in groups of four. As you listen, note down in your own way any words or phrases which you still do not understand. Then compare notes with others in the group. Try to help each other with these problems. Finally, check any remaining difficulties by reading through the transcript on pages 67–72.

Unit 8   One-upmanship

Pre-listening

1 Before listening to the tape, look carefully at the notes below.
  They were made by the director of a chain-store company
  who is interviewing candidates for a junior managerial post. In
  them he has noted down the qualities etc. he is looking for.
  Make sure you understand them before going on to the listening. It will be helpful for you to discuss them with a partner.
  Try to form a mental picture of the ideal candidate.

Memo for interview re. junior manager's post

Experience
At least 3 yrs in management of small family business
or small store or similar.

Age
Late 20s early 30s.

Status
Single/no family problems.
Need for free transferability through U.K.

Personal qualities
Honesty.
Energy.
Loyalty to the firm.
Tact.
Must get on well with people.

Salary
Negotiable £2500–£3500 according to experience.

Listening

2 a) Now listen to conversation 1 on the tape. You will hear two of the candidates talking to each other after the interview. From what you hear and the way you interpret it, what can you deduce about them regarding the points the manager was looking for?

Points to look for	*Candidate A*	*Candidate B*
Experience		
Age		
Status		
Personal qualities – honesty – energy – loyalty to firm – tact – getting on well with people		
Salary		

Some of the information is present in the conversation, that is, it is stated by the speakers. Much of it however, you will have to make guesses about on the basis of the attitudes/qualities you feel are being expressed. You will need to listen to the conversation more than once.

b) Now compare your ideas in groups of three. Then check them with another group.

3 a) Now listen to conversation 2 on the tape. Do exactly as you did for conversation 1. That is, record as much of the information needed for the manager's points as you can hear or deduce.

Points to look for	Candidate A	Candidate B
Experience		
Age		
Status		
Personal qualities – honesty – energy – loyalty to firm – tact – getting on well with people		
Salary		

b) Again discuss it in groups of three, then compare your ideas
with those of another group.

4 a) On the basis of the information you have gathered about
these four candidates, which one do you think has the best
chance of being offered the job? (It may help you to know
that in the first conversation one of the men was an assistant
supervisor in Woolworth's for two years with a staff of five.
This may change one or more of the judgements you made
about him.)

b) If you had to choose one of the people as the pleasantest and
one as the most unpleasant who would you choose? Why?
Discuss this in your group.

c) In each of the two conversations one of the speakers was in-
dulging in 'one-upmanship', that is, he/she was trying to
make the other person feel inferior. Which two people were
trying to be 'one-up' on the others? How did they do it?
You will need to listen to the tape again and stop it whenever you come to a sentence in which you can hear it
happening.

5 Which of these pictures correspond with your idea of the people you heard speaking on the tape? Discuss your choice with a partner.

Intensive listening

6 There are a number of idiomatic phrases in both conversations. The meanings of these phrases are set out below. Listen to the tape again and stop it each time you come to a phrase you recognize as having one of these meanings. Write it down in the space provided.

Meaning	*Words used on tape*
She has trouble with her legs.	
Would not be very useful.	
A great deal/very much.	
I direct the work of . . .	
My flat is in the same building as the shop.	
Anything is possible.	
In addition to.	
How well did you do?	
I hope the person who deserves the job will get it.	
Quite well.	
You're quite mistaken.	

Check your answers, first with a partner, then with the teacher.

Checking up

7 Listen to the tape again in groups of four. As you listen, note down in your own way any words or phrases you still do not understand. Then compare notes with the others in the group. Try to help each other resolve these difficulties. Finally, check any remaining problems by reading through the transcript on pages 73–5.

Unit 9   Exit 13

Pre-listening

1 Look at the road map on page 38, and at the Automobile
Association's (A.A.) advised route from Bristol to Upton-
upon-Severn below. Using the A.A. guide, trace the route on
the map. Does this seem to be the best route to take? Discuss
possible alternative routes with your partner.

> Urban at first then joins M5 Motorway for 42m, through
> pleasant undulating, partly wooded country (occasional
> views of the Severn Estuary) with the Cotswold Hills
> to the right. Later through flatter country with the
> Malvern Hills on the left.

Miles		
		BRISTOL
		Follow signs **Gloucester** A38
		to leave by Gloucester Rd
		In 7m at rbt take 3rd exit (**SP Midlands**)
		to join **Motorway M5**
7.5	7.5	Junction 15 (M4)
15.5	8	Junction 14 (B4509)
17.7	2.2	Michaelwood Service Area
26	8.3	Junction 13 (A419)
29.2	3.2	Junction 12 (A38)
38.7	9.5	Junction 11 (A40)
46.5	7.8	Junction 9 (A438)
50.2	3.7	Junction 8 (M50)
		Branch lt **M50** (**SP South Wales**)
51.7	1.5	Junction 1
		Leave Motorway (watch your speed)
		(**SP Malvern**)
		& at rbt take 2nd exit **A38**
		(**SP Worcester**)
		In 3m t lt **A4104** (**SP Malvern**)
		In 1 m cross R Severn
56	4.3	UPTON-UPON-SEVERN

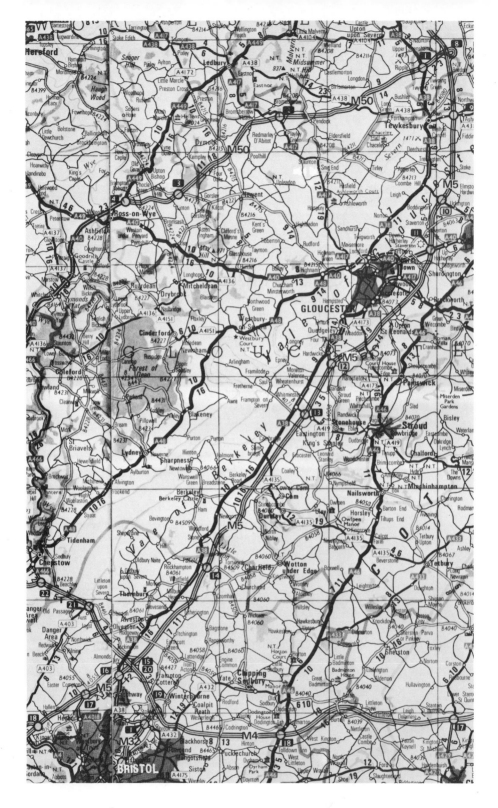

Listening

2 a) You will now hear a conversation between two people, one
of whom wants to take the A.A. route, the other of whom
wants to use an alternative route of his own. As you listen
fill in the grid below with details of the alternative route and
the reasons he gives for wanting to go that way.

Alternative route	Reason

The man makes a mistake when reading out the road
numbers. What should he have said instead of A41? Check
the map for yourself and make this correction before
proceeding to exercise 2b.

b) When you have finished compare your notes with a partner.
Do it in the following way:
You look at your grid and he looks at the map. You then
give him directions based on your notes and he has to trace
the route on the map. As you give directions, give the
reasons too (e.g. Then he decides to take the A41 to Stroud
because of the music festival). ✈—◔

Intensive listening

3 a) The woman is rather pessimistic and cautious about
accepting the new route and she uses several arguments
against doing what the man suggests. Listen to the tape
again. As you listen, number the arguments listed in column
A in the order in which you hear each one.

	A	B
Waste time eating.		
Miss turnings and waste time.		
Must not drink and drive.		
Get stuck in traffic.		
Lose way on new routes.		
Get sick through map reading.		

b) Now listen to the tape again. This time stop each time you come to one of these points and write down *exactly* what she said in column B. You will probably need to listen to the tape more than once. Discuss your notes with the teacher and the rest of the class.

Checking up

4 Listen to the tape again in groups of three. As you listen, note down in your own way any words or phrases which you still do not understand. Then try to help each other with these problems. Finally, check any remaining difficulties by reading through the transcript on pages 75–7.

Pairwork

5 Below is a letter giving rather confusing instructions on how to travel from Upton-upon-Severn to Coleford. Working in pairs, one of you should read the letter silently and then give instructions to the other, in your own words, regarding the route from Upton-upon-Severn to Coleford. The other should then listen to the instructions, take notes and trace the route on the map.

After checking change roles. The student who was taking notes, should now give instructions to the other for taking the motorway route via Ross-on-Wye. Once again, the route should be traced onto the map and afterwards checked and compared with the instructions.

23, Twig Lane,
Coleford

Aug. 25th 1981

Dear Jim and Margaret,

Your uncle and I are very pleased you can join us next week-end for the birthday celebrations.

So, just to make sure that you have no problems getting here, I thought I would send you these directions. I hope you will be able to follow them without too many problems.

I suggest you take the main Gloucester Road from Upton. I can't remember the number but I'm sure you must know the one I mean. Be careful, however, to avoid Gloucester city centre. You can do this by taking a right turn just before entering the town, and, if you do that, you'll also get a marvellous view of the Cathedral.

A couple of miles along this road there is a fork. I usually take the left fork towards Minsterworth, but your uncle insists on continuing straight till Huntley and left to Mitcheldean.

You must choose but if it's a nice evening, I'm sure you will enjoy the route via Minsterworth, and you can then rejoin the A4136 at Nailbridge or you could turn off left at Cinderford and take the backway to Coleford.

Your uncle has just leant over my shoulder to read this and says that you might prefer to take the motorway route via Ross-on-Wye, but we shall leave that choice to you.

Have a good journey.

See you soon.

Auntie Mabel and Uncle George

Unit 10 Left out?

Pre-listening

1 Divide into groups of three or four to discuss the following advertisement. Do you recognize the characters? Do you know the story behind the picture? What is the caption really saying? Do you think it is effective? What other caption would you have chosen to go with this picture?

When you have discussed these ideas within your group, try to remember a situation when you think you were left out or not fully informed. What consequences did it have for you and the other people involved? How did you feel about it? Share your ideas about this with other members of the group. Follow up your discussion in a class discussion with the teacher.

Listening

2 Now listen to version 1, dialogue 1. In pairs, try to work out:
   i)   what the relationship is between the two speakers.
   ii) how old they are.
   iii) whether speaker B has been invited or not.
   iv) what speaker B really means when she says, 'I'm afraid I couldn't make it tomorrow anyway.'
   Listen to the dialogue several times if necessary. Then discuss and compare your ideas with another pair. ✂–◑

3 Now listen to version 1, dialogues 2 and 3. This time, again in pairs, try to work out:
   i)   whether the first person to speak in each dialogue is the same person in both dialogues.
   ii) who the first speaker is.
   iii) why the first speaker in each dialogue is so interested in finding out the reaction of the person who was not invited.
   iv) what the other person's reply was in each of the dialogues. (Do the two replies agree?)
   v)   which of the two replies best fits what was actually said in dialogue 1 (listen to dialogue 1 again if necessary).
   vi) what the motivation of the person replying was in each case, i.e. why did he/she reply in this way?
   vii) how the first speaker reacts to the replies.
   You may need to listen to the dialogues several times again before you can answer all these points. ✂–◑
   When you are satisfied with your replies, discuss them first with another pair, and then with the whole class and the teacher.

4 Now listen to version 2, dialogue 1. Do exactly as in exercise 2 above except that this time you should discuss what speaker B really means when he says:
   'I'm afraid I can't make it er byebye.'
   Again discuss and compare your ideas with another pair. ✂–◑

5 Listen to version 2, dialogues 2 and 3. Answer the same points
as in exercise 3 above. Once again discuss your replies with
another pair, then with the teacher and the whole class.

Intensive listening

6 a) Turn to pages 78–9 and read through the transcripts of the
dialogues. Then listen to the dialogues again. As you listen
try to match some of the adjectives below with the attitudes
conveyed by the speakers. (There may be more than one adjective per speaker.)

Version 1 dialogue 1 speaker B
Version 1 dialogue 2 speaker C
Version 1 dialogue 3 speaker E
Version 2 dialogue 1 speaker B
Version 2 dialogue 2 speaker C
Version 2 dialogue 3 speaker E

anxious	indifferent	amused
disappointed	hurt	concerned
annoyed/frustrated	offended	worried
satisfied/smug	frivolous	upset
uninterested	gossipy	insistent

When you have finished compare your answers with a
partner. ⚷

b) Make sure you know the meaning of these idiomatic
phrases:
  – I can't make it.
  { – He took it quite well.
  { – He took it all in good part.
  – He spilt the beans.
  – He was dead choked.
  – You could see it written all over his face.
  – One of those things.
  – He will open his big mouth.
  – Bloody Hell!
  – She tried to shrug it off.
  – Serves her right. ⚷

7 On the basis of what you have understood about the eight
speakers in the two versions, try to match them with the
pictures on page 45.

Checking up

8 Listen to the tape again in groups of four. As you listen, note down in your own way any words or phrases you still do not understand. Then compare notes with the others in the group. Try to help each other resolve these difficulties. Finally, check any remaining problems by reading through the transcript on pages 78–9.

Pairwork

9 Discuss in pairs what B in version 1, dialogue 1 might say to C in dialogues 2 and 3 when they next meet, and how C might reply. Then try to act out the situation – one person taking the role of B, the other of C. Do the same for another pair. Discuss the kind of language you needed to use with your teacher.

Unit 11 Football crazy, football mad

Pre-listening

1 Divide into small groups of three or four. Think back in the past to a situation (which you are willing to share with the others) where for some reason you agreed to do something and then changed your mind.
What was the situation?
Why did you want to get out of it?
What did you do or say in order to get out of the situation?

When you have done this, try to think of a situation (which you do not mind relating to the other members of your group) where you have had to break some bad news to someone.
What was the news?
How did you break it?
What did you do/say exactly?

Listening

2 a) Now listen to telephone conversation 1. A football team manager, Alan Russell, is telling a player that he will be dropped for Saturday's match. While the recording is being played the first time listen simply to see how he goes about it. How does this correspond with the way you would have done it? (From 1 above.)

   b) Now listen to the tape again. This time, note down in column 1 of the grid all the excuses the manager tries to find for excluding the player and, in column 2, the counter arguments given by the player.
   Do not worry if you do not get all the information the first time. The tape will be played again.
   Now listen to the tape once more and concentrate on collecting information for columns 3 and 4 of the grid. You

Excuses	Player's counter arguments	Real reasons	Player's reaction
i) Trouble with leg.			
ii)			
iii)			
iv)			

may write down the exact words of the speakers in these columns if you wish. When you have finished, compare your ideas with a partner. Finally, build up the completed grid on the blackboard with the teacher. 🗝

3 Now listen to telephone conversation 2. This time the manager, Alan Russell, is talking to Bob, the player who will be replacing John. In the course of the conversation the manager tells several lies about what happened in the previous conversation. Try to note these in the grid below, along with what actually happened.

Manager's lies	What actually happened
i) 'I told him straight.'	
ii)	
iii)	
iv)	

Listen to the tape as many times as you need to. Then discuss your notes with a partner. Finally, the teacher will collect all your ideas. 🗝

4 a) In conversation 3, you will hear the two players, John and
 Bob, talking to each other over a glass of beer. John also dis-
 torts the facts about his not playing for the team. He does
 this in two ways.
   i) By finding reasons for not being able or not wanting to
       play.
   ii) By lying about what went on in his conversation with
       the manager (Russell). Try to record this information in
       the grid below:

Reasons for not playing	Lies about telephone conversation
i)	
ii)	
iii)	
iv)	

Listen to the tape as many times as you need to. Then compare your ideas with the others in the class by having the
teacher build up a completed grid on the blackboard. 🔑

b) There is a major inconsistency between what John says in
 the course of the conversation and what he says at the very
 end. Can you detect what it is? 🔑

Group work

5 a) Work in groups of four. Each group will work as two pairs.
 Look back at exercise 1. Choose one of the situations (or
 another similar one if you prefer). Each pair should act out
 the situation as a role-play for the other pair to observe. The
 pair who are not acting should note down any points they
 think could be improved. These can then be discussed.
 It may be useful to discuss with the whole class what you do
 – when you want to:
 apologize
 make a tentative or indirect suggestion

request someone to do something
ask for clarification
pacify or calm someone down
threaten or warn someone
– or when you are:
embarrassed
regretful
disappointed
angry

b) If there is time, go back over the tape of telephone conversation 1 and find examples of the way some of these things were expressed there.

Checking up

6 a) It may be helpful to listen out for the following phrases, many of which have an idiomatic meaning.
– 'A bit of new blood.'
– 'Experience counts.'
– 'I'm only human.'
– 'I might as well tell you.'
– 'Let's be frank.'
– 'If you don't mind my saying so . . .'
– 'It's a dead loss.'
– 'Cards on the table.'
– 'I told him straight.'
– 'Goodness knows what.'
– 'Did he take it hard?'
– 'He's getting on a bit.'
– 'You're standing in for me.'
– 'About time.'
– 'The team isn't up to much.'
– 'You can't have it both ways.'
Discuss the meaning of these phrases with your group and with the teacher if necessary. ☛—○

b) Listen to the tape again in groups of three. As you listen, note down in your own way any words or phrases which you still do not understand. Then try to help each other with these problems. Finally, check any remaining difficulties by reading through the transcript on pages 79–83.

Transcripts

Unit 1 Sleeping habits

Interview 1

A. Good morning sir.
B. Good morning.
A. Would you mind if I asked you a few questions?
⎧ We're doing a . . .
B. ⎨ Well I'm in a bit of a hurry.
A. market survey.
    Well it won't take very long, really.
B. Well, all right.
A. . . . be very grateful.
B. What's it all about?
A. Umm, well it's about your sleeping habits.
B. My *sleeping* habits?
A. Yes. Um . . .
⎧ Just a few questions
B. ⎨ It's a bit personal.
A. We . . . well we'll try and keep it – decent.
    Um – how much time every day do you spend um making the bed?
B. Well I don't make the bed. My wife makes the bed. She's always made the bed.
A. I see. Oh.
B. I don't think men should be making beds, do you?
A. Does she spend a long time doing it?
B. Oh we've got one of those er 'duvet' things. I think you just throw it over.
A. I see.
B. Ha . . . She makes a lot of fuss about making the bed but er . . .
A. So not very long?
B. Not very long, no. I suppose about a minute or so.
A. Hm. What do you um do before you go to bed in the evening?
B. Well I er, well, ha that's a bit difficult isn't it?
A. Ha, ha.
B. I suppose er I read – sometimes.
A. Mm mm.
B. Sometimes I just flake out like that.
A. Mm. Mm. Thank you.
B. Er. Sometimes. Yeh, sometimes you know, talk and er mess around, you know . . .

51

A. Mm. Mm. And um, whe . . . when you wake up in the morning do you . . . what is the bed like?

B. What's the bed like?

A. Hm.

B. What do you mean, what's the bed like?

A. Um. Well I mean is it . . .

B. Well. Looks as if somebody's been sleeping in it.

A. I see, yes.

B. All wrinkled, isn't it?

A. Very, very untidy?

B. Well not very untidy. I, I'm quite a quiet sleeper so they say.

A. Hm.

B. My wife isn't.

A. Hm. Your wife isn't?

B. No. Her side of the bed's always in much more of a mess than mine.

A. I see. Do you um, do you sleep well at night?

B. Oh yes. Straight out. No trouble at all.

A. But if, if you have a problem or if you can't sleep, what do you do?

B. If I have a problem? Well I um, try not to think about it I suppose.

A. I see, yes. You don't have a method for going to sleep?

B. Oh well, the old counting sheep and that?

A. Mm.

B. No, I just er try and think of something else you know.

A. I see. And um, supposing . . . do you er wake up sometimes in the middle of the night?

B. No, never. Well, unless somebody comes to the door or the telephone rings, no never.

A. Oh. I see. And, supposing you hear a strange noise in the night, what do you do?

B. Well ah. I'd go down and have a look round.

A. Very brave.

B. No. I'd erm, I'd just be angry I think. Being disturbed. Worried about the house, you know.

A. Mm. Mm.

B. Wife to look after. Children . . .

A. Mm. A responsible husband. And um, do you . . .

B. Well I suppose you could say that, yes.

A. Do you have er complaints? Do people um, are people angry about the way you sleep?

B. I haven't had any complaints to date. No.

A. None at all?

B. No. I'd say I'm a very nice person to sleep with. Easy. Anything else?

A. Yes. The last question sir. Um. What sort of dreams do you have?

B. Well. Don't dream much actually.

A. Never?

B. Um. No. No. Can't say I dream. No, not very much.

A. What was the last dream you had?

B. Oh well. I always try and remember them when I wake up, if I've had a dream, and then it just goes . . .

A.   Mm.
B.   I used to try writing them down or talking about them but my wife
     doesn't seem very interested now. Says my dreams aren't very
     interesting.
A.   Oh dear. Oh.
B.   So, er, well anyway.
A.   Well maybe, maybe you could tell me about them? Anyway, then . . .
     Thank you very much sir . . .
B.   Yeah maybe I might do that.
A.   Thank you. Yes.
B.   Right.
A.   Goodbye.
B.   Goodbye.

Interview 2

A.   Good morning sir.
B.   Er. Good morning.
A.   I wonder if you'd like to answer a few questions?
B.   Well er . . .
A.   We're doing a market survey.
B.   depends what sort of questions they are ah?
A.   Well it's questions about your sleeping habits.
B.   Sleeping habits?
A.   Mm.
B.   Well. I suppose that's all right. Yes. Well. What do you want to
     know?
A.   Right. Um. What would you do if you heard a strange noise in the
     middle of the night?
B.   I'd wonder what it was er I suppose and then I'd um see if it happened
     again.
A.   Mm.
B.   I would lay awake a little while, waiting to see if it happened again, and
     if it did – I suppose I'd get up . . .
A.   Mm.
B.   and go and see what it was.
A.   Very courageous. Um. If you, if you can't get to sleep at night, er, what
     do you, what do you do? Have you a special method?
B.   Well I generally go to sleep straight away. I don't have any trouble
     getting to sleep.
A.   Mm.
B.   Well if I do have . . . occasionally, happens about once every six months
     I suppose that I can't go to sleep and then I er I lie awake and I um think
     about things.
A.   Mm. Mm. Think about things. And er what about before going to bed?
     What do you do before you go to bed?
B.   Well I, depends, er if I've been out I, I, don't do anything, I just come
     home and go straight to bed. I clean my teeth. Ha. Ha.
A.   Mm. Good. Good.

B. That's one thing I do before I go to bed. Um, well I occasionally read a bit but if I read I go, I tend to go straight to sleep. I, I, can usually read about a page and then I go straight off.

A. Mm. Yes. Me too. Yeah. And um when you dream, what do you dream about?

B. Aah! Now that's a *very* interesting question.

A. Mm.

B. Yes. I've been dreaming a great deal recently as it happens.

A. Have you?

B. Mm.

A. Have you?

B. Um. I've had dreams every single . . . all, all the way through my holidays, I've just come back from my holiday and I've been dreaming every single night. Quite worrying dreams. Very worrying dreams. For example, I had a dream about parrots the other night.

A. Parrots?

B. Yes. Green parrots. I mean, they shouldn't have been there because it, we weren't in any tropical country or anything.

A. Er. No. No.

B. It was a flock of parrots.

A. A flock?

B. A flock. A whole flock of parrots.

A. That's funny.

B. And there I was climbing up this stream bed . . .

A. Yes. Um.

B. with these parrots flying around. Ha. Most extraordinary.

A. Really. Yes. Would you describe that as a nightmare?

B. Well it's rather worrying don't you think?

A. Very – Well, um, another question sir. How much time do you spend making your bed every day?

B. I don't spend any time at all. I just get out and then I get back in, in the evening.

A. I see. So no time at all. And, um. Yes the last question, um have you had any people complaining about your sleeping habits?

B. Complaining?

A. Yes
⎧ That's to say . . .

B. ⎨ What would they complain of?

A. D'you, perhaps you snore at night?

B. No I don't snore.

A. Perhaps you, you talk in your sleep.

B. No. I, I tend to take up rather a lot of room though.

A. Yes. I can see that.

B. Yes. Yes. I do tend to use up more than my fair share of the bed, yes.

A. But you . . .

B. Roll around a bit.

A. But you've had no complaints?

B. Well, I occasionally get complaints but I don't take much notice of them. What can you do?

A.   Yes. Quite so. Well um, thank you very much indeed sir. You've been very co-operative and helpful.

B.   Yes. Well thank you. Yes. It was quite interesting speaking to you actually. Ha. Ha.

A.   Goodbye.

B.   Byebye.

Unit 2   Good buys

M.   Here we are darling. I think I've got all the stuff for you.

W.   Oh super.

M.   Aah. Dear me. Wet out.

W.   O.K. Let's er . . . Well better get it unpacked quickly and get it all put away.

M.   Right. Now, what have I got? Er, some cream here.

W.   O.K. Fine.

M.   I could only get single but you didn't actually specify on the list, I think, what you wanted.

W.   Ooh dear! Well I, well I suppose yes I can beat it up with some sugar and egg yolk or something and make it thicker. What else have you got here now?

M.   Strawberries I've got.

W.   Yeah.

M.   But just a few because they were a bit expensive.

W.   How much were they?

M.   These?

W.   Yeah.

M.   Mmm. Would you believe 40?

W.   Well, all right. O.K.

M.   Here you go. Now, ah, pièce de résistance. Here we are – chicken. It's quite a big one.

W.   O.K.

M.   Four pounds eight ounces. That do?

W.   Hmm. Well, I suppose if it was the best you could get, it was the best you could get. What else have you got? Did you get the tomatoes?

M.   Yes. They're somewhere down here.

W.   Fine.

M.   There we are. Here are the tomatoes and . . .

W.   Well thank you for putting them under the chicken. They'll be squashed now.

M.   They won't. They're very firm.

W.   Well, they'd better be.

M.   Hmm. Mushrooms. Yes, we managed the mushrooms. There are the mushrooms are there . . .

W.   O.K.

M.   and, oh, onions. I had a problem with onions, I must confess. Spanish onions, I didn't know what they were, but um I got these little ones. Are these any good to you?

W.	No dear! They're pickling onions.
M.	Oh.
W.	I'm sorry. I mean they've got totally the wrong flavour. Completely the wrong kind.
M.	Well, I suppose in another ten minutes I can go back and try and find some.
W.	Would you?
M.	I'll do my best.
W.	Well all right love. Thanks.
M.	Anyway there's some more things here to unpack. Er, rice. Here you are. Packet of rice.
W.	Er. That . . . no, no, no, no, no. That's short grain rice.
M.	Oh. Is there a difference?
W.	Yes dear, I wanted long grain rice for savoury cooking and you've got pudding rice.
M.	Oh! Well it'll taste just the same surely? Oh well.
W.	It doesn't look the same though, does it?
M.	I know. I know.
W.	Oh well.
M.	If you can make do . . . There's a lettuce at the bottom here somewhere. Oh dear! Yes it has got a bit squashed. I'm sorry about that.
W.	I asked you to get me a crisp lettuce.
M.	Well er.
W.	Oh!
M.	These looked very good, so I got what I could.
W.	⌠ Yeah. Well.
M.	⌡ Sorry about that.
W.	Oh well, all right. Did you get the oil?
M.	Aa, yes I did. But I couldn't get olive oil. I've got this vegetable oil. Olive oil, they just didn't have.
W.	Oh, darling no.
M.	Unless you bought great big tins of the stuff.
W.	Yes I know but look. I mean it's far better to buy a large quality olive oil – a large quantity of olive oil because the quality's so much better.
M.	Well how far do you think the housekeeping's going to go? I mean let's face it, that oil is very, very expensive.
W.	Well I know it is but . . . it's so much better.
M.	I think you'll have to make do with that. Wine vinegar I've got too.
W.	O.K.
M.	Here you are, er how about that?
W.	Did you get the herbs?
M.	Oh. No.
W.	Well you'd better put that on your list with the onions.
M.	Oh dear. Herbs, onions, er yes um . . .
W.	Bread?
M.	Bread. Yes, there's a . . . where have I left it? Oh, I've left it outside . . . a whole . . .
W.	What do you mean, you've left it outside?
M.	Well, I've left it in the hall.

W.   Oh, all right. O.K.

M.   Fairly long loaf of bread for you er and that's about it I think.

W.   Where's the cheese?

M.   Oh, don't say I haven't [sic] forgotten that as well. Tch. Oh well . . .
    ⎰ cheese.

W.   ⎱ You've not left it on the counter, have you?

M.   I think I have you know. I'm sure I paid for it. Gorgonzola . . .

W.   (sigh)

M.   Never mind, I can go back. I've got,
    ⎰ what eight minutes left . . .

W.   ⎱ I don't know why I don't go and do the shopping myself.

M.   Well I wish you would. I wish you would.

W.   But you did offer to help.

M.   Well I've got you some things. At least you can be going on with
    something, can't you? You can be starting the first course or something
    like that, can't you?

W.   Oh for goodness sake
    ⎰ go and get me those onions.

M.   ⎱ Well look I must just . . .
    Yes. All right. I'll go.

Unit 3   Know yourself

M.   Oh well, what about this then, eh? Umm . . .

W.   What are you looking at?

M.   Loving . . . loving, yeah . . . um . . .

W.   Oh, well I'm definitely, yes I'm definitely very, very loving. I mean I
    wouldn't be sitting . . .

M.   Very?

W.   Oh yes, extremely, outstanding. What are the different categories?

M.   Well, you've got er . . .

W.   Outstanding . . .

M.   Yeah?

W.   Outstanding I'd say . . .

M.   Well, I wouldn't say that. I don't think. Its dangerous to say you're
    outstandingly anything.

W.   Well, I've put up with you for the past ten years.
    ⎰ And you have to be outstanding to do that.

M.   ⎱ Well, that's fairly outstanding. Why don't we just . . . can't we come
    to some sort of agreement? I mean er . . .

W.   Well, above average then . . .

M.   Above average . . .

W.   Selfish . . .

M.   Yeah . . . er . . .

W.   ⎰ selfish
    ⎱ I think we ought to fill this thing in about you actually. You'd rate as
    outstand . . .

M.   No, no, we're filling it in about you.

W.   { That's a bit one-sided.
M.   { I reckon . . .
       what do you reckon? Tell me what you think.
W.   Selfish? Me? I'm not selfish at all.
M.   I didn't s . . . I didn't say you were. I said um how?
W.   Poor. I'd put poor for that one.
M.   No, I think you're about average.
W.   Give me an example of that!
M.   Well, poof, well, what about when we want to watch the television eh?
W.   Well . . .
M.   Who . . . who wins? Which channel eh?
W.   Well, I do, but that's only because you . . .
M.   Aah . . .
W.   You don't know how to pick your programmes, I mean er . . .
M.   Well, yes, but I'd call that selfish. I think I'd call that selfish.
W.   You never have time to read the
      { television programmes
M.   { No, no, I don't think you're, I don't think you're, I don't think you're
      outstandingly selfish, but I don't think you're . . . I wouldn't say poor
      either, I'd say average.
W.   Oh, that's quite good of you.
M.   I mean you're averagely . . . I mean everyone's averagely selfish, aren't
      they? Even me.
W.   I suppose so. Well, all right then, average. Hey! Have you seen the next
      one?
M.   Sexy? Huh! . . . Huh!
W.   D'you think we've got to fill that in?
M.   Sexy? . . . Yeah!
W.   Oh . . . well . . .
M.   I'd say outstanding for that. What would you say?
W.   Oh, well if you say so . . .
M.   Well. I do. I think you know, well I think we'd better pass onto the next
      one actually, yeah . . .
W.   Loyal.
M.   Loyal?
W.   Oh yes, oh yes, I'm ever so loyal. Remember when I stood up for you
      against your brother Archie the other week, when your mother was
      getting at you? I mean I, I stood up for you then didn't I?
M.   But what about um . . . what about . . .
      { Mrs er . . . Mrs Jones next door?
W.   { What about . . .
      What about Mrs Jones next door?
M.   Well, what about what I heard you saying about me over the garden
      fence last week. I wouldn't call that very loyal, would you?
W.   Well, I, I, I was, I was just trying to make a point to her.
M.   Yeah well, you could make your point somewhere else, couldn't you?
W.   Well, you shouldn't listen to other people's conversations.
M.   Well, I don't see why you should go we . . .

W.	⌠ washing your dirty linen in public.
	⌡ Well never mind about that. We'll put average down for that.
M.	Oo . . . er. I think I would put well all right er . . . really should be below average but er . . .
W.	Rubbish, rubbish, rubbish!
	⌠ You shouldn't have been listening.
M.	⌡ Well all right, O.K. All right.
W.	Anyway, jealous.
M.	Jealous.
W.	Never.
M.	Oh, yes.
W.	I've never been jealous.
M.	What!
W.	I've got nothing to be jealous of, have I?
M.	What about when you saw, what about when you saw me talking to my secretary outside th . . . the office the other day and you thought I was, I was dating somebody eh? Didn't even know it was my new secretary did you, eh?
W.	Well.
M.	What about all that fuss you made?
W.	Well, it's just that you don't take the take, ttt the, you don't pay the same attention to me, that, that's all. I wasn't really
	⌠ jealous . . .
M.	⌡ But why should I pay that sort of attention to you anyway? I'm married to you, aren't I?
W.	Oh, you cheeky so and so! What do you mean?
	⌠ You should, should pay attention to me. I'm your wife.
M.	⌡ Well, there you are you see . . . well, you are jealous, you, you are jealous. Above average. Jealous. I should say. Even outstanding. What do you think?
W.	I disagree. I disagree. You've got it all the wrong way round.
M.	Well . . . I think we should come to some sort of agreement. I mean . . .
W.	No, no, I'm not jealous. I think below average, definitely below average.
M.	Well, I'll show you.
	⌠ Well all right I'll . . .
W.	⌡ I, I was just taking an interest in your friends the other day, when I saw you with that . . .
M.	I'll show you how loyal I am by agreeing with you. All right?
W.	All right. Below average.
M.	O.K.
W.	Secretive.
M.	Hoo . . . hoo!
W.	Secretive.
M.	Above average. Outstanding!
W.	What do mean? I show you . . .
M.	Secretive?
W.	I show you all the letters that come through the letter box.

M.   All the ones I see coming through the letter box, yeah. What about the others?

W.   What 'you talking about?
       { You know there's only one delivery.

M.   { The second delivery.
       Huuh . . . what d'you mean only one delivery?

W.   Well, there is . . .

M.   And what about the postman eh?

W.   What about him?

M.   Well . . .

W.   Well, well, I've got the right to have a little chat now and again haven't I?

M.   Yeah, well I . . .

W.   After you and your secretary. I mean you can't say that I haven't got a right to, to, to . . .
       { have a little chat with Fred.

M.   { Yeah . . . but what about all that, all that business with your sister last year as well, eh? Whipping off for . . .
       { the afternoon to the sauna.

W.   { Now listen here! Just stop digging things up will you?

W.   No, no,

M.   Eh? That was pretty secretive, wasn't it? Eh? Going off to the sauna bath . . .
       { and, and massage every, every Wednesday.

W.   { I'm not doing, I'm not doing this sort of thing if you're going to dig up all the past.

M.   Eh? Every Wednesday afternoon . . .
       { without telling me?

W.   { You're spoiling my . . . you're spoiling my Saturday afternoon.

M.   And what about when I asked you about it? You didn't exactly come into the open did you?

W.   Well, let's put average down, come on, and finish this off . . .

M.   Below, below, I think.

W.   Finish this off and count up the points.

M.   Below average.

Unit 4   Flat hunting

J.   Well, it's really nice of you Brenda to er . . . invite me to stay until I find this flat, but I'd really like to try and find something. Have you got any suggestions?

B.   Well, let's have a look in this paper, here.

J.   Let's see.

B.   Erm.
       You're looking for a two bedroom place, aren't you?

J.   Well, yeah preferably.

B.   Because your son might be coming to visit you sometimes.

J.   Yeah, yeah.

B.   Erm . . .

J. Well, of course, I'll be working in Kensington, so . . .

B. In Kensington, well let's see . . .

J. So within striking distance.

B. Can you see anything? There's something here in Chelsea, that's not too far away.

J. Chelsea, let's have a look.

B. Let's have a look at that one. Three rooms, kitchen and bathroom. That's O.K. isn't it? Wonder why they say, 'Ideal Overseas Visitors'?

J. Prob . . .oh . . . £80. That's why! Charge you the earth for it!

B. Is that more than you can afford, uh?

J. Yeah, besides it's short lets available, so . . .

B. Oh, you'd want something long let, wouldn't you?

J. Yeah, yeah.

B. Let's see what else there is. Bayswater . . . Bayswater's not too far from Kensington as well.

J. There's no tube though, is there?

B. That's quite cheap, isn't it, £50?

J. £50, well, er I er . . .

B. That's not bad for London.

J. D'you think so? I was, I was thinking of spending . . .

B. Well, what is it? It's a double, single . . .

J. Large . . . what's that . . . large reception room,
⌠ kitchen, bathroom, long let.

B. ⌡ Large reception room, that's not bad you know. I mean, I'll tell you. You have to look at some of the other ones and you'll find that er, you can't do much better than that.

J. Well, £50 still strikes me as pretty expensive.

B. Let's, quickly run your finger down the page.

J. Ah, Kensington Church Street, that . . .

B. Well, that's £60. There's one. The Angel £37.

J. The Angel.

B. That's quite a long way away from Kensington, you know.

J. What's . . . what's the tube? Is that direct or not?

B. The tube from the Angel to Kensington High Street, no, no.

J. Let's see . . .

B. No, Angel's on the Northern Line.

J. Yeah, you'd have to go Northern Line and then take the Circle Line wouldn't you, so it'd involve at least one change.

B. That's not too bad.

J. Yeah, I suppose, but it's all the same during rush hour. I've done this before. It's really pretty unpleasant.
Let's see . . .

B. Mmmmm . . . but, I mean, you won't get anything . . .£37, I mean, I don't . . .

J. That's, that is a definite advantage.

B. It is cheap, and it's furnished too.

J. Yeah, washing machine as well. Amazing, yeah, well, O.K. That's something to bear in mind. But, let's have a look, is there anything else? Marylebone High Street.

B. Here, this is an amusing one in Hampstead. It's got ornithological views. Er, are you interested in bird spotting?

J. Oh, depends what kind of birds of course, but er . . . .

B. Ah, ha!

J. Yes, but, er, well let's have a look at this.

B. I don't think that's what they've got in mind.

J. No, probably not.

B. Oh, it's only April to October. But it does say preferably academics which . . .

J. Yeah . . . that . . . erm . . .

B. I wonder why that's April to October though.

J. Oh, no. That's, that's central heating.

B. Oh, I see. Oh, central heating is April to October.

J. Yeah, they heat from April to October.

B. That can't be right.

J. No, surely not!

B. Oh, it's when . . . Oh I don't understand that advertisement.

J. No, better leave that, besides, that's £65.

B. £65. Can you see anything cheaper? Er, no, I think that's it really.

J. Yeah.

B. One in Hyde Park. If you want to live around Hyde Park, you've got something for £100 a week. How about that?

J. Well, thanks a lot!

B. Two double bedrooms . . . looking over the park. Can't you afford that?

J. Well, if you're working at
⎰ the er university . . .

B. ⎱ I'll tell you what, I think you'd better er . . . which ones shall we mark that you ought to phone?

J. Well, the Angel, I suppose.

B. The Angel, and I reckon you should try this Bayswater one.

J. D'you think so.

B. Yeah, that sounds quite good.

Unit 5 Getting there

A. I was thinking about our holiday this summer.

B. Yes. I'm looking forward to it.

A. Well –

B. It's going to be lovely driving out there . . .

A. Colleague at work showed me this er advert here.

B. Oh yes.

A. I thought it looked very interesting. Think we might have to change our plans.

B. Why? I don't see any reason to change our plans at all.

A. Well he says that er he and his wife last year went by ship down to Spain.

B. By ship!

A. Yeah.

B.   Oh. You'd be sea-sick all the way.

A.   Well he said they had a lovely time. Never had such a relaxing holiday.

B.   I don't believe that at all. What, what's relaxing about being on a boat?

A.   Well he said you, you, you just sat there and you let things happen, and they go to all these marvellous things happening on board.

B.   Such as?

A.   ⎰ Well, you can go the the cinema. You can just sit in a deck-chair.
B.   ⎱ Oh I bet they show you old films all the time.

A.   Well maybe they don't. Not these days I'm sure. Probably got a choice. And then er, well you can just sit and watch the sea going past and er ⎰ read . . .
B.   ⎱ Well that's very boring isn't it. If you take the car, you've got, you've got the freedom of the road, you can see the countryside . . .

A.   Freedom of the road!

B.   Yes.

A.   All that pollution. Think of all the fresh sea air blowing in.

B.   Yes. All you see is the sea and then you get sick, and then you, you can drive off the little roads, visit the villages, visit the churches, the cathedrals and . . .

A.   And how long's that going to take?

B.   Well, you can take as long as you like. You're quite free to, to spend a long time doing it. Anyway we did it last year and I . . .

A.   And look what it cost us, before we even got there.

B.   ⎰ Well how much does it cost . . .?
A.   ⎱ Stopping off in hotels, Going off to see this and that.

B.   Well that's because we didn't book. But if you book ahead, and book ⎰ nice cheap hotels, that'll be all right.
A.   ⎱ They don't have cheap hotels on the motorway.

B.   Yes they do. Well, you drive off the motorway.

A.   Well I like the idea of just paying a lump sum and there you are, you've got everything – all your food, all your cabin. You get everything – drinks are cheap.

B.   Drinks are cheap, well you can, you can get cheap drinks in France anyway. No problem.

A.   And then think about the children. Much more fun for them. There's a nursery and they can go and play games on the deck . . .

B.   ⎰ What sort of games?
A.   ⎱ They'd like the cinema. Well they've got these um, what's it called here? Quoits.

B.   Quoits? What's that?

A.   No I, I, He was telling me about it. It's a thing you, you've got these round things and you whizz em along. A bit like bowls, except they're flat.

B.   Quoits, I see. What else can you do?

A.   Well they've probably got lots of other games too, and there's a swimming pool too.

B.   Hm. Well you could swim in the Lot can't you? Swim in the rivers.

A.   Well, you can . . .

B.   When you're going down on the, on the motorway.

A. Yeah but there's always somebody tells you, 'you can't swim here'.

B. Mm.

A. What's that sign they have there in, in French, I don't know? Anyway it says 'No swimming'.

B. Well.

A. Well, I don't know. I, I think this is much better, you know, last time we, we, by the time we got there we were exhausted, and then we'd spent everything we had . . .

B. Yes. Well. I, it's not really very expensive you know. I'm sure the boat costs a fortune.

A. Yeah and then . . .

B. And you, you'd be drinking all the time. You'd be at the bar all the time, spending all our holiday money on duty-free whisky. I know you.

A. We'd be meeting some interesting people.

B. ⎰ But you don't meet any interesting people.

A. ⎱ Didn't meet anybody . . .
    Well we didn't meet anybody in the car, did we?

B. Whew.

A. A few angry drivers. And then remember what happened then?

B. No.

A. Nearly had an accident going down, trying to drive on the wrong side
    ⎰ of the road. Right side for them I suppose.

B. ⎱ Well, yes. I mean, hah – that wouldn't happen again.

A. And you remember all that trouble we had trying to get the petrol when they had that petrol strike? And going into the garage and trying to get that puncture fixed up, and I couldn't speak a word of it.

B. Yes. Well I've got a phrase-book this year, so that's no problem.

A. Got a phrase-book. Well that's not going to help us, why don't we just go with sort of ordinary English people and talk to them on the boat?

B. Mm. Well I still think we should go by car because when we get to Spain, we want to travel around by car, and, and we won't be able to see anything if we haven't got the car with us.

A. Well er. If we haven't got the car *with* us?

B. Yes.

A. But we can take the car with us.

B. We can take the car?

A. We can take the car with us. Says here 'book your family and car'.

B. ⎰ On the boat?

A. ⎱ And travel direct.
    Yeah. Yeah. You put your car on, so, if you want to do all this freedom of the road business, you can do it when you get there.

B. Oh. Well . . .

Unit 6   Missing plans

Call 1

A. Hello?

B. Hello, Anna?
A. Yes.
B. Hello my darling, it's Bob.
A. Oh, hello darling.
B. How are you?
A. I'm fine, how are you?
B. Good, I'm all right. Listen, I've worked out what I'm going to be doing for the next couple of weeks.
A. Yeah.
B. Erm, I'll be down here in Bristol from Monday to Thursday because ⎰ I've got full time lectures all all during the day.
A. ⎱ Yeah, O.K.
B. Then Thursday, I've got a couple of days off, so I'm going up to Mum's at Leeds and I'll be staying for the weekend.
A. Oh, well, do you have to . . . you can't get back by Saturday, can you? 'Cos we've been invited to this super party and it would be nice to see you,
⎰ d'you think you could?
B. ⎱ Yes, well, I'll be up on Saturday, erm, but I've got to come back to Bristol on the Sunday.
A. Oh, er, early? I mean, you can, you could sleep in can you? 'Cos, it's rather a late party. You don't have to get up early, do you?
B. Er, well, that, I'm not sure about yet, because I've got to find out the er, train times and er, obviously, I've got to get back Sunday night.

Call 2

A. Hello?
B. Er, could I speak to Bagshot, please?
A. Er, this is Alan Bagshot speaking.
B. Er, hello, it's Johnson here. Er, just filling you in with my itinerary for the week.
A. Oh, yes, yes.
B. Er, now, I'm in London at the moment and er, tomorrow – Monday, I'll be going down to Bristol and visiting a chain-store down there.
A. Oh, yes.
B. Tuesday, I'll be driving over to Wales. I'm going to Cardiff, er, to the branch office.
A. Oh yes, that'll be to see Mr Sutcliffe, won't it?
B. Indeed. And I'll be sorting out a few local problems there with him.
A. Fine.
B. And I shall be leaving there after lunch because I shall have quite a journey, well, fairly heavy journey. I'll be going on to Birmingham and I want to get to Birmingham on the Tuesday evening so that I rest up overnight. I'll be spending Wednesday at Birmingham.
A. Hm, hmm.
B. And I'll be staying overnight at Birmingham on Wednesday.
A. Yes.

B. Thursday morning. I'll be driving straight off to Manchester to visit the factory
{ and er, to see the new designs.
A. { Oh good, yes well we'll look forward to seeing you then.
B. Well, I'll be able to call into the office for erm, half an hour or so, and er, have, discuss a few points with you. And then Friday night I'm not sure whether I'll stay on in Manchester or whether I'll be going on to Leeds and er, there's a des . . . new designer in Leeds I want to have a chat with er, he's sent me some designs erm, but in any case, I'll be going to the Lake District on Saturday visiting
{ friends.
A. { Yeah.
B. Unless my wife comes up to Leeds to visit her mother.
A. Oh, I see that's fine er.
B. In which case, I'll be staying there.
A. Tremendous, well, I've got most of your details down and er I'll look forward then to seeing you, on er, on Thursday, is it?
B. On Thursday, yes, and I'll clarify everything with you then. All right? Bye.

Call 3

B. Hello.
A. Hello, Alan?
B. Yes.
A. Oh, it's Geoff, here.
B. Oh, 'allo.
A. Er, I just wondered whether er, you could do me a favour?
B. Oh, what's that?
A. Well, er I've got some er, some goods I'd like to have taken down to er, to Hull.
B. Yeah.
A. I wonder whether I could er, chance it, er if you could do er, a job for me?
B. Er.
A. Well, I'll give you an idea of of of what I'm, what about. You see, on, on Monday, I've got to go down to Hull, the warehouse.
B. Yeah.
A. But then on Tuesday, I'm going to Nottingham, 'cos I've got to pick up these parts and then I've got to take 'em up to Birmingham. That's on the Tuesday, you see.
B. Yeah, yeah.
A. Er, but er, you see the following day, the lorry's er, got to come up to Manchester again for servicing.
B. I see er, do, do we make the trip together er to pick up the parts and go down to Birmingham on Tuesday?
A. Er, well, we could do, if that's all right with you.
B. { Yes, that's all right, yeah.
A. { Er, that'd be fine. Erm anyway, going on a bit, erm, where've we got

66

to, Wednesday, Thursday, no Thursday, I've got to go to the Liverpool docks with some stuff.

B.   Yeah.

A.   But er, now this is me problem. Friday, er, I've got to go up to Glasgow, but erm, unfortunately, er, something's come up, like er, Manchester City. Manchester City is er, well is playing Sheffield in Sheffield and er, you know, I'd er, being a keen supporter and all that, I wonder if you'd care to take the trip for me?

B.   Er, to Glasgow.

A.   Er, well, I know it's er a lot of time and all that, but er would it be possible d'you think?

B.   Well, you want me to do you fu . . . to go to Glasgow, so you can watch City?

A.   Well, er.

B.   Er, ah, I, if it was United, I'd do it,
    ⎰ but . . .

A.   ⎱ Oh . . .
City, bloody hell, I mean . . .

B.   You cheeky monkey, you che . . .

A.   You will now, now come on, now you will now, won't you . . .?

B.   Yeah, of . . . , well, I think I can do that. I mean er what time in the morning?

Unit 7   Great expectations

M.   Morning, Brenda.

W.   Good morning, sir.

M.   Er, did you, did you put that, that ad. in yesterday?

W.   Yes.

M.   The junior sales manager.

W.   Yes, it went into the Standard and the Evening News.

M.   ⎰ Jolly good. Erm, well . . .

W.   ⎱ What kind of person have you got in mind for this job?

M.   Oh, well, somebody fairly young, you know 21, 25, that sort of thing.

W.   Hm, hm, hm, hm.

M.   Man, I think.

W.   A man?

M.   We really need a man. Yes, I mean, it's, it's really too demanding. The sort of situations that they get into are much too difficult I think for a, for a young woman to deal with, erm . . .

W.   Erm, what sort of a young man had you got in mind?

M.   Oh, you know, a good education, er I, what I don't want is is one of these young cocks of the walk, you know just out of university with exaggerated ideas of his own importance
    ⎰ and . . .

W.   ⎱ hm, hm.

M.   and how much he's going to
    ⎰ earn. Frankly.

W.   ⎱ Hmmmm.

M. I mean, I'm not er prepared to er to give him a very big salary to start with. I mean the increases he gets in his salary are, are going to be dependant on on on how er how effective he is. Er . . .

W. Yes, erm, what sort of education are you actually ⌠looking for?

M. ⌡Well, you know, a couple of A levels. Must have English of course.

W. Yes.

M. But er, somebody who's er ready to to start working er and and to to get on because of the work he does, er, ⌠well, someone with a nice way with him really . . .

W. ⌡Yes, how are you going to . . .

M. Someone with a nice, nice manners and er . . .

W. I think you're asking quite a lot.

M. Good accent, you know, I don't want somebody who talks like a gutter. Erm, asking a lot?

W. Yes, I think, you're asking quite a lot. ⌠I mean you're not really prepared to pay all . . .

M. ⌡Well, I don't think so . . .

W. that much, but you want someone with a good education whose . . .

M. But not a degree.

W. Nevertheless, a good education, but polite and and tactful, you you don't want erm someone . . .

M. Want someone ambitious, actually.

W. Yes.

M. Someone with plenty of ambition, plenty of drive.

W. Mm.

M. You know, mmm, not looking at the clock all the time.

W. Are you going to be prepared to pay them overtime?

M. Well not in . . . not initially. Er, er, he'll get a bonus.

W. Well sir, I wish you the best of luck and I hope that you have some very successful interviews.

M. Well, yes.

W. Because, personally, I think you're asking an awful lot.

M. Well, you know a single man.

Candidate A

C. Good morning.

M. Er, good morning, yes, er . . .

C. I'm phoning about the job that was in the paper last night.

M. Oh yes, yes, erm, well, could you tell me your name, please?

C. Oh, Candida Fawcett.

M. Oh, yes. Erm, well what exactly er is it that interests you about the, about the job?

C. Well, I just thought that it was right up my street you know.

M. Really, hmmmm. Erm, well could you perhaps tell me a little about yourself?

C. Yes, erm, I'm 23. I've been working abroad, I um . . .

M. Where exactly have you been working, please.

C.   Oh, in Geneva.

M.   Oh, really.

C.   Yes.

M.   And, what were you doing there?

C.   Oh, secretarial work.

M.   I see.

C.   And erm, previous to that, I was at university.

M.   Hmmm ... hm.

C.   And erm ...

M.   Which university was that?

C.   Oh, the University of Manchester, I've got a degree in English.

M.   Hmm, hmm. And er, you're interested in the job?

C.   Oh yes sir, really, I am. Erm, can you tell me what it's paying?

M.   Er, well, I think that would be negotiable erm, if we decide to invite
     you for interview then I should er, I should er, er talk to you about that,
     but perhaps you could give me an idea of what sort of er ...

C.   Oh, I'm n ...

M.   What sort of er range you're interested in.

C.   I'm not really too worried about getting a ... er ... large salary to start
     with.

M.   Really.

C.   It's just that I should be, you know, very happy, to be able to have a job
     to come back to England and work and erm ...

M.   Do you have any special reasons for wanting to come back?

C.   Well, it's just that with being, working in Geneva for a year and, I sort
     of thought it would be nice to be nearer the family, you know.

M.   I see. Yes. And er, how do you see this job developing?

C.   Well, I am ambitious. I, I, you know, I do hope that my career as a
     secretary will lead me eventually into management or, or ...

M.   I see. You, you have, you have foreign languages, I take it?

C.   Oh yes sir, yes sir, French and Italian.

M.   Oh yes, hmmmm. Well, look. I think the best thing for you to do is to,
     is to reply in writing to the advertisement and er ...

C.   Oh, can't I arrange for an interview now?

M.   Well, I'm afraid, we we must wait until all the, all the applications are
     in, in writing and er, er we'll then decide er on a short list and er, if
     you're on the short list, of course we shall see you.

C.   Oh, I see.

M.   Yes, so, I'll look forward to receiving your er, your application in
     writing in the next day or two.

C.   Oh, yes, yes, certainly.

M.   Yes, thank you very much, goodbye.

C.   Thank, thank you. Goodbye.

Candidate B

M.   Hello, Pharmex?

C.   Hello, could I speak to the er personnel ma ... manager, please?

M.   Yes ... speaking.

C. Ah, er, I'm phoning up about this job you've advertised in the paper. This er, er, young sales manager.

M. Oh yes, yes hmmm.

C. Erm, I'd like to apply for it. D'you, what happens, d'you send me 'a' application form?

M. No, er you simply, you simply apply. You simply er send in a written application, a letter.

C. Oh, right erm, can you tell me a bit more about it please, erm? I mean, er, what sort of job it is, er.

M. Well, we're really looking for someone er, er, who is er, anxious to get on er, and who er, is not er, too concerned about working fairly long hours. Erm.

C. Oh, long hours, what, what, d'you mean by long hours, I mean?

M. Well, this is a job which does have er, as the advertisement says, it does have travel possibilities and
⎧ er . . .
C. ⎩ Yeah.

M. and very often this means that er, one would be away at weekends for instance.

C. Oh I see, er, oh I thought you meant working in the evenings and er . . .
⎧ working overtime like.
M. ⎩ Well, it could also mean working in the evenings but er, well for a managerial post, I'm afraid we don't pay overtime. Erm, that's for other grades.

C. Oh, er, I see, what, what kind of money are you paying then?

M. Well, this is to be negotiated. Er, it depends partly on your experience and and education. Perhaps you could tell me very briefly er, what that is.

C. Yes, well er. I've just left school
⎧ and er . . .
M. ⎩ I see . . .

C. I've got A level, erm . . .

M. Er, A level?

C. Yeah.

M. Er, in what?

C. Er, er, geography. Um . . .

M. Oh, I see and and in English?

C. Er, no, no, I . . . I didn't get English. I . . . I got O Level in English.

M. I see, yes, hmmm.

C. And er, it's th . . . the long hours though working in the evenings, I mean, yeah, it's the travel that appeals to me, this is why I'm er enquiring about the job.

M. Yes, I see. Well, look perhaps I could, er what . . . what sort of er what sort of a salary were you thinking in terms of? Perhaps you could tell me that.

C. Well, er, starting off, I thought it would be something like 50 quid a week or er something like that. You see.

M. Oh I see, yes, well, erm, look perhaps I could ask you to do er what the

70

advertisement says. That is

C. ⌠to say er to . . .
  ⌡ Yep . . .

M. send in a written application er and then we'll consider your case along with all the other applicants.

C. All right. Thanks very much.

M. Yes, thank you goodbye.

C. Bye.

Candidate C

M. Hello, Pharmex.

C. Oh, erm, hello, I'm I'm ringing in connection with er, your advertisement

M. ⌠ er, in the paper.
  ⌡ Oh, yes, hmmm.

C. Box 222.

M. Yes.

C. Erm, I would er rather, well, I'm I'm rather interested in applying for this job. I don't know whether I have the correct qualifications but er . . .

M. Well, perhaps you could tell me what your qualifications are.

C. Well, er, I'm er, a young man. I'm I'm 25, I've er, just got married.

M. Oh, I see, yes erm.

C. And at the moment I'm studying er, chartered accountancy, er, er, er, I'm not yet chartered of course, but er . . .

M. How long do you er expect to take over that?

C. Well, I should take another year in fact. But er, I wondered in fact whether I'd be suitable for your job. You see, I I I have worked in a sales department before. I worked at a toy factory.

M. Oh yes.

C. But er, unfortunately, er, the way things go I I I was made redundant.

M. Oh I see, yes, erm.

C. But er, you know I I feel erm.

M. Can you tell me something, I er, something about your educational background? Are you er . . .?

C. Oh, well, A levels basically.

M. Hmmm.

C. Mostly, sort of scientific

M. ⌠ subjects . . .
  ⌡ Yes.

C. But er . . .

M. Do you have English?

C. Er, yes, I do.

M. Oh you do, yes ah ha.

C. You see, I feel, I I I'd like to sort of get on er really, but er, you know I I need a bit more experience,

M. ⌠ before er I . . .
  ⌡ Yes, experience of what exactly?

C. Well er, I suppose you could put it down to er responsibility. You know, I need to feel my way around a bit before I can, I'd actually sort of er . . .

M. This would be a, this would be a fairly responsible position from the outset in fact.

C. I see.

M. Hmm . . .

C. Erm.

M. What sort of er, what sort of a salary were you thinking of?

C. Well, could I ask what sort of salary you're offering?

M. You could ask but I'm asking you.

C. Oh I see er, well, I I'd of thought something round about er oh, 4000.

M. Hmmm I see. You say you've just got married?

C. That's right, yes, yes.

M. Yes, and does your wife work?

C. Er, she doesn't at the moment, no. But, er, she she's erm she's thinking about it.

M. I see. Er, you do note that there is a considerable er travel element in this job.

C. Oh.

M. Would that, er . . .

C. Yes, I didn't realise that
⎰ erm, but of course . . .
M. ⎱ Well.

C. It does say, it does include travel. Er would that be immediately

M. Well, er, fairly immediately, yes.

C. Oh.

M. It's difficult to predict, because it depends on the demands of the job.

C. Yes, yes, er, well I understand that. Erm, yes
⎰ well . . .
M. ⎱ Well, look, perhaps I could ask you to er to complete a written application and . . .

C. Well yes certainly, if you could do that, if you could send me something er on paper that we, we could, we could talk further about, you know erm.

M. Well,
⎰ I think, I think it's for you to send it to me actually.
C. ⎱ This'd be fine.
Oh, yes.

M. You send a written application in and we shall then er be be drawing up our short list in the next week or two.

C. Right. I send it t . . . to this address, do I?

M. That's right, yes.

C. The one that's on the card here.

M. Box 222.

C. Right, thank you very much anyway.

M. Thank you, goodbye.

C. Goodbye.

Unit 8   One-upmanship

Conversation 1

A.   How d'you get on then?

B.   Oh – fairly well, thank you. Yes, yes, fairly well. You?

A.   Hoo . . . Can't complain. Can't complain.

B.   Good.

A.   Seemed to go very well indeed, I must say. He seems er . . .

B.   Yes?

A.   A very nice fellow.

B.   Oh yes. Indeed. Yes, well it's a firm with a good reputation isn't it?

A.   Well. It's manage . . . er, manageral [sic], whoop – can't say the word – managerial experience is what they're looking for, isn't it?

B.   Er. Yes. Yes. Yes.

A.   You had any of that?

B.   Er, yes. You could say that. Yes. I've been you know running my own business.

A.   Aha. I, of course, I had a big staff, I had, 'cause I was at er Woolworth's, you know, I was supervisor for er two or three years, er, had a whole shop under me, which is rather nice.

B.   Well I mean, yeah I – there's only a couple of us and and family helped out . . .

A.   Er, mm. Mm.

B.   So, not a great deal of staff but I don't suppose there's any difference, is there, between . . .

A.   Oor. Er! Don't you believe it mate. You want to . . .

B.   two or twenty, I mean. Same problems.

A.   Well you wait till you get them all – coming up for you.

B.   Yes I hum, looking forward to, I mean, you know working for a big firm rather than working for yourself. All that paperwork you have to do for the government nowadays is . . .

A.   Yeah. Must say er he seemed er reasonably generous in what he was going to offer. I thought er 3000 to start with was quite er quite acceptable.

B.   Oh er 3000 he said did he? Oh yes. Yes; yes, yes it's er yes very generous.

A.   You er you married by any chance?

B.   Er yes. Yes. Yes.

A.   Oh yeah. So you got er got some family ties and things have you?

B.   Yes. We, we've er we er own the house, er next door to the shop.

A.   How you going to find travelling then? Travelling's going to be a bit of a problem for you, isn't it?

B.   Well no, I don't think so. I mean, there's a very good train connection em well what do we live, what, 20–22 miles away but er still I should, you know, just means getting up early in the morning to travel in . . .

A.   Yeah well

B.   and er can't really move because er got um illness in the family you see.

A.   Ooh.

B.   Yes. My mother.

A.   Sorry to hear that.

B.   She's not so well. You know she kept on working on in the shop but er her legs are playing her up a heck of a lot so . . .

A.   Ooh. Sorry to hear that. Anyway er may the er may the best man er win in this case I suppose really.

B.   Certainly. Yes. Yes indeed.

Conversation 2

A.   'ello. How d'you get on then?

B.   Oh. 'ello. Oh, all right. Yes. Yes. He seemed quite nice really didn't he?

A.   Yes, I suppose so. What've you been doing up till now?

B.   Oh, I've got a little family business, you know, just a, just a small business with the, a staff of two, you know a . . . and my mother of course.

A.   ⎧ Mmm.

B.   ⎩ she works with me, just small but I, I, I like it that way. He, he, he seemed quite interested I thought.

A.   Yes I'm an assistant supervisor.

B.   Oh really.

A.   I'm at Woolworth's you know at the moment. I've been there for two years.

B.   Really?

A.   Staff of ten under me. Mm.

B.   Oh.

A.   Before that I was with the Co-op in the grocery department.

B.   Oh. You're quite experienced then, aren't you? Yes . . .

A.   Oh yes I'm very experienced.

B.   He, he must have er been impressed by that I suppose.

A.   ⎧ Oh I expect he was, yes.

B.   ⎩ Yes.

A.   And there were my references of course.

       ⎧ Yes you see,
B.   ⎩ Ah oh yes . . .

A.   ⎧ I suppose you can't really bring references when you've got a family
       ⎨ business can you?
B.   ⎩ Well not really, no. No it's rather difficult isn't it, I mean, I mean my mother's reference that wouldn't be much good would it?

A.   Well . . .

B.   ⎧ No, I don . . .

A.   ⎩ I don't expect it would.

B.   He seemed to understand that though, I thought. You know he, he didn't seem to mind.

A.   No. No. How d'you feel about being asked about overtime though?

B.   Oh well, I, I don't mind that really because of course in my own shop, shop you know I have to do overtime. I mean, it's, it's really you know
       ⎧ living on the premises, you know, that sort of thing.
A.   ⎩ Mm. No I like putting my coat on at six o'clock and going out and forgetting about it. Ha. Ha.

B.   Yes.

A.   ⌠I mean my social life – you know . . .

B.   ⎨Yes. Yes. I expect you would. Yes.

A.   ⌡Yes. Yes.

      Did he ask you if you'd mind going to another district?

B.   Well er yes yes. I, I, don't mind, you know I don't mind really I . . .

A.   Oh I don't mind as long as he's going to pay the same money. I thought

      ⌠that was uh a pretty good offer, really you know.

B.   ⌡Well actually you see um well there is one trouble though of course.

      ⌠I er we we've got our own house and that might make it a bit difficult.

A.   ⌡Oh yes.

A.   Oh yes.

B.   Could I get transport? That would mean – yes that's slightly difficult I, I um . . .

A.   Oh I don't know. They don't like putting transport allowances, not on top

      ⌠of a good wage like that you know.

B.   ⌡Oh no, no. Well I wouldn't expect that, no.

A.   Mmm.

B.   I don't know really, yes.

A.   Mm.

B.   Have to think about that.

A.   Anyway, ha, ha, you know what they say – ha 'May the best man win'.

B.   Ha. Yes. Yes.

A.   ⌠Or in our case may the best woman win.

B.   ⎨Ha. Ha. Yes.

A.   ⌡Yes. Yes. Well, it's been nice meeting you.

B.   You too, yes.

A.   Yes. Yes. You never know he might take us both on . . .

Unit 9   Exit 13

M.   What've you got there then

      ⌠the A.A. guide? What's that, an itinerary?

W.   ⌡Yeah, I think this is the way we should go. Yes. 'Cos it's terribly, terribly simple this way,

      ⌠you see.

M.   ⌡Mmm mm!

W.   It's going to, if we, if we go . . .

M.   It's all M5 motorway, that's

      ⌠ridiculous.

W.   ⌡Yeah, well I know that's why it's good, because it's going to sort of take us only a few hours

      ⌠and . . .

M.   ⌡Nooo!

W.   we're going to . . . what?

M.   Well look, we're in no hurry, er in fact, I've worked out a very very good way of getting there . . .

W.	{ up to Upton. { Oh I know your way of getting to places, { we always lose our way,
M.	{ But the . . .
W.	{ you know what it's like.
M.	{ No, we don't . . .
W.	And also, I have to read the map too and that makes me feel sick in the car.
M.	Well look, I've prepared this, there's no problem look . . .
W.	{ Oh well, O.K. you tell me . . .
M.	{ If we, take the look . . . ah now look here, if we take the A38 up to about what three or four miles off Gloucester we can then get on to the A41.
W.	But can we? You know what it's like, we never do.
M.	Well we can.
W.	We spend hours missing our turning.
M.	Look, look, A41, if we get off erm exit 13, A41 takes us to Stroud.
W.	Yes, { what's there?
M.	{ There's a musical festival on at the moment { in Stroud.
W.	{ Well, you imagine how crowded it's going to be. We're going to get stuck with all { those damned hippies.
M.	{ Well, everybody'll be inside the music festival.
W.	Oh no, they
M.	{ they'll be all lining . . . { Oh no, it's a posh music festival. Oh yes, it's not hippies.
W.	Oh, oh well.
M.	Anyhow on from Stroud. Then, if we go up to Painswick we can have lunch there 'cos it's a beautiful little village, smashing I mean there are . . .
W.	But it's going to take, you know, hours and it's oh, I don't know.
M.	You haven't seen the pub, I'm going to take us to.
W.	Is it { nice, I mean not . . .
M.	{ Marvellous! { what food? { You know . . .
W.	What sort of things?
M.	Beautiful sort of fresh country bits and pieces.
W.	Oh mmm mmm . . . that's the kind of thing that . . .
M.	Very good beer.
W.	tempts me, I must say.
M.	Aha, now onwards, { we go to . . .
W.	{ (Laughs) A bit tempting. We can't drink too much though, 'cos we're driving, you see.
M.	Well that's fair enough, but you'd like it there { I'm sure you would.
W.	{ O.K. . . . well . . .

M. There's a loo there for you if you're interested. (Laughs.)

W. (Laughs.) Oh well, I'm always interested in that, you know what I'm like.

M. (Laughs.) Onwards to Gloucester on the
⎰ B4073.

W. ⎱ This is a g . . . we're getting so complicated.

M. It isn't, it isn't. I mean, I know this road very very well. And in fact when we get to Gloucester, we could buy Mum's present there . . . that plate she wanted.

W. Oh, yes O.K. but it . . . (sighs).

M. As long as it's not an early closing day, it'll tell you
⎰ the early closing days in the book.

W. ⎱ Oh . . . oh will it? Oh!

M. Er . . .

W. It always is . . . If the weather's ghastly, you know it's going to be so horrid. The pretty way is the lovely way, when the weather's nice, but you know . . .

M. Now, A417 out of Gloucester.

W. Yeah,

M. Then if we go on the B4211, now, that takes us to Snig End Tea House.

W. (Laughs) What's that . . . Sn . . .

M. Haven't you been there?

W. No.

M. I'm sure . . .

W. It sounds a funny place.

M. I must have gone with some other woman. (Laughs.)

W. Oh, you horror.

M. Ah dear, no it's a beautiful little place. Erm, again we can get erm tea there, gingerbreads and all sorts of things.

W. Oh, you're beginning to tempt me, I must say. All this food.

M. Well, it's much better than the M5. Those motorway
⎰ restaurants and service areas are . . .

W. ⎱ Well I know, I wasn't thinking of eating there, I was thinking of sort of taking my own stuff. I mean I could take a nice picnic.

M. Well, you see we've got an alternative after we've had our tea there. We can go on the A417 to the M50
⎰ to Upton that's if we're sort of . . . a bit pressed for time.

W. ⎱ Yeah.   Mmmmmm.

M. Or we can take the B4211 and carry on on the sort of . . . on a minor road.

W. Well yes, you are
⎰ beginning to tempt me.

M. ⎱ That depends really on the time factor involved, you know, if we are really pushed for time there.

W. We
⎰ could . . . .

M. ⎱ But I reckon that's by far the best way of going.

W. Yeah, well O.K.

Unit 10 Left out?

Version 1 dialogue 1

A. O.K. then, bye. Oh, I suppose I'll see you at Alex's tomorrow?
B. Where?
A. At Alex's. Haven't you been invited?
B. Oh Alex's. Oh well, I'm afraid I couldn't make it tomorrow anyway.

Version 1 dialogue 2

C. Were you there when Angela asked Barbara if she was coming tonight?
D. Aah. Yeah. I think I was. Yes.
C. What did she say?
D. Well, I mean, she simply asked if, er, if she was coming to you and er she said 'no' and she said she couldn't make it, that's all.
C. She a – she wasn't upset or anything?
D. Not that I could see. No.
C. Bloody hell!

Version 1 dialogue 3

E. Did you hear what Barbara said when Angela asked her if she was coming tonight?
F. Yes. She was terribly upset. She really was.
E. Was she?
F. Yes.
E. What did she say?
F. Well I mean she tried to shrug it off – you know how she is – but I mean – she was really hurt.
E. Good. Serves her right.

Version 2 dialogue 1

A. O.K. then. Bye. I I suppose I'll see you at Alex's tomorrow?
B. Where?
A. At Alex's. Haven't you been invited?
B. Oh. Er, Alex's um ye yes well I I I'm afraid I can't make it er byebye.
A. Ooh, bye.

Version 2 dialogue 2

C. Oh you must tell me what happened. Did, . . . oh, no tell me, now tell me – what happened? How did he take it?
D. Oh he didn't seem to mind. Why, why should he? Really. He seemed to take it quite well.
C. Oh goodness. Oh it's so funny you see. I didn't want to invite him. I had no idea that anyone would say to him, 'Are you going to be at Alex's tomorrow?'

D. Oh don't worry. I think he took it all in good part.
C. Are you sure?
D. Yeah honestly. I really don't think he minded.

Version 2 dialogue 3

E. Sid, you were there when Andy spilt the beans about tomorrow, weren't you?
F. Oh yes. Yeah.
E. What was Bob's reaction?
F. Oh. He was dead choked.
E. Oh no!
F. Oh yes. You could see it written all over his face. He was really cut up about it. Tch. Well, one of those things isn't it? I mean, you know, Andy will open his big mouth.
E. Well, I know.
F. He's got no tact, that bloke, at all. I mean Bob was really upset you could see that.

Unit 11   Football crazy, football mad

Conversation 1

A. Hello? Hello, John?
J. Oh, yes, hello, you wanted me to call you.
A. Yeah. Hello John. Yeah I, I just er just wanted to talk to you about er about this er about the match on Saturday.
J. Oh yes. Oh yeah! Now what sort of position are [sic] you fancy I shall be playing?
A. Well you know. I was wondering . . . you, you've had a bit of trouble with your leg you know I, I, I wonder, I thought perhaps you might like to lay off this week and um . . .
J. Well.
A. Give your, give your ligament a bit longer to . . .
J. Yeah I know.
A. to mend.
J. Well I spoke to the, to the team doctor and he wasn't, well wasn't too worried about it. He thought, you know,
  ⎧ it ought to er have a bit of exercise.
  ⎨ See . . . I should be playing again.
A. ⎩ Yeah, but, but I was thinking I was thinking too you know it's, it's a bit of a, it's a bit of a distance er you know we're playing away.
J. Mm.
A. Playing Denham. That's quite a long way away and um, I know you work on Saturday morning, you know I thought may be . . . it'd be a bit difficult for you to er . . .
J. Oh, that's all right. No, I could er, I could make up the hours. There's no problem there, I mean overtime's no problem for me.

A.   Oh yeah I know, but I mean. You know Denham's not a very strong . . .
     it's a pretty weak team er . . . just wonder if it's worth the energy, you
     know.

J.   Oh, I don't know. I mean that team they won er, let's see they they
     played last three matches they, they won two of them didn't they?
     They, the last match they played was at . . . the other weekend . . . they
     drew.

A.   I know, but they're, they're pretty weak er . . .

J.   It was against Brentford!

A.   pretty weak er opponents each time I think . . . tch well you know I, I
     was just wondering whether we shouldn't try out, you know, one or
     two of the . . . you know some bit of new blood? Yeah?

J.   I dunno, we are . . . I think the, the way we're playing at the moment
     you want to keep the team we've got! I mean, let's face it, I mean
     experience counts. I mean you got a . . .

A.   Well . . . you know I've I've been getting, problem is I've been getting a
     bit of, you know pressure from the supporters you know, they, they,
     they seem to want a bit of want to see some new talent and . . .

J.   ⎰ Well . . . wha . . . what . . .
A.   ⎱ You know, younger players and . . .

J.   But what what are you trying to say? Come on, I mean huh, I'm, I'm
     only only human, I mean you . . .

A.   Well look, yeah, well look I might as well tell you, I mean, thing is, I
     think we're going to have to, we're going to have to, to drop you this
     week um I mean you, you haven't been scoring, your goal average is is
     very low this year and . . .

J.   Well I . . . .

A.   and frankly, frank . . . I mean I, let's be frank, you know I mean er, I've
     got, I've had some complaints, I mean the the number of times you've
     been you you've been fouling recently.

A.   Well I, I think this is absolutely unjustified, if you don't mind my saying
     so because, I mean, I think, I mean I play I play as hard as as any of them,
     I mean . . .

A.   Well yeah, I know you do, I, I mean, I know you do.

J.   Look, now look. I think this is ridiculous. I mean, I . . .

A.   Well look. The thing is I, I, look I, if, if you can be dropped this time, I,
     I mean we can, we can give you another chance . . .

J.   Aa . . . oh!

A.   later in the season.

J.   Ah . . . oh no! Stuff it! I mean this is, this is stupid. I mean I've been
     playing as well as any other man in the team and you ought to know
     that, I mean, this is . . .

A.   There's nothing I can do about it John, I mean.

J.   Pfuf! All . . . I think your team's a . . . well it's a dead loss anyway, I've, I
     . . . I, I don't bloody care if I ever play for you again. Let's put it like that
     straight. If you want, if you want cards on the table, that's it.

A.   Well, don't take it like that eh . . . ?

J.   No, I'm sorry, I feel this way.

Conversation 2

A. Hello Bob?

B. Hello yes?

A. Hello. Hello. It's Alan here.

B. Oh hello Alan.

A. Yeah well, I got a piece of good news for you actually.

B. Yeah?

A. Yeah. We got you a place on the team.

B. What for this coming ma . . . Saturday?

A. ⌠Yeah, yeah.

B. ⌡Saturday's match?

A. Well I've rung up John.

B. Yeah.

A. And, you know, I told him straight, you know, I told him, you know he, it's no good, he's, he's, his goal average is down, he's he's always kicking people in the shins and goodness knows what so I just told him that, you know, as far as I'm concerned er we, we drop him.

B. Right. So I'm playing?

A. That's right.

B. Fantastic!

A. Yeah, yeah.

B. What what did he say to that then?

A. Oh well you know, in fact he was quite reasonable. You know, I mean, he, he said he understood that we couldn't go on you know,

B. Yeah . . .

A. We couldn't go on . . . and anyway he's got to work on Saturday morning.

B. ⌠Yeah. I mean er . . .

A. ⌡And er,

B. ⌠did he, did he take it hard because he's . . .

A. ⟨No, no, no.

B. ⌡done some pretty good work for the team, hasn't he?

A. No, no. He was very reasonable. I was very pleased actually. He took it very well.

B. Ah, good.

A. And er, you know well in, in future, you know, I er, really it looks as ⌠though he's, he's dropped out, you know, he's, he's, drop . . .

·· B. ⌡What, how long for?

A. Well I don't think we can really think of, of taking him back now. He's getting on a bit and er . . .

B. Well I mean he's had that injury, that, er,
⌠that's going to last a few more weeks really . . .

A. ⟨Yeah, yeah, yeah, so.

B. ⌡To clear it up totally but er. What do you, what do you mean? He's not going to play again or . . . ?

A. Well I, I, I don't think that we can really er think about taking him on again um you know he's he's getting on in years and er . . .

B. { Oh that's pretty bad luck.
A. { I think it's better if we just er leave it like that now. So anyway you got your place on the team for next Saturday.
B. Oh fantastic, Yeah!
A. So er, you know, er, there it is, O.K.?
B. O.K. That's great. Yeah.
A. So I'll see you, I'll see you down at the stadium on Saturday then.
B. Right I . . . you going to have usual training practices before, training sessions?
A. Yeah but I probably won't be there on Wednesday but er anyway I'll see you on Saturday, O.K.?
B. O.K. Fine, great.
A. Bye.
B. Bye.

Conversation 3

J. Aah! Good drop of beer that. Aah!
B. Again?
J. Er, yeah, I don't mind. I'll have half.
B. Well how are you?
J. I'm all right.
B. Good, how's the leg?
J. It's fine. Why shouldn't it be?
B. Well. No reason. I was just . . . yeah I mean er you haven't been playing for us for a couple of weeks er . . .
J. Yeah well, takes a wh . . . a while to heal doesn't it? You know.
B. Yeah. Yeah. I do.
J. Can't er do too much exercise on it, can I?
B. No.
J. See you're er you're standing in for me then this week eh.
B. Er yeah, oh yeah, yeah, I got a game this Saturday, yeah, ha.
J. Eeh. Well.
B. It's good eh? About time. I mean I've been in reserves for a long time. Mind, mind you, I mean er you know, I don't enjoy like to take away a game from you.
J. Well I can hardly play, can I? Anyway, the er, the team isn't up to much these days I reckon.
B. What do you mean?
J. I'm er, you know between you and me, I'm er not really planning to stay very much longer.
    { You know the er . . .
B. { Why's that?
J. Humph. The club record is er is not terribly good is it?
B. Well I mean it hasn't, we haven't been playing so well for the last few weeks because you've been off out of it with your leg.
J. Well . . .
B. Well it takes time to get better, I mean . . .
J. Well it's, it's the general team spirit of the thing you know I, I warned

Russell you know I spoke to him on the phone the other day and er . . .

B. Yeah?

J. I've warned him for some time that this was going to happen. I was . . .

B. Well I mean if you haven't been playing with us obviously the team's lost something it's er . . .

J. ⌠ Al . . . always . . .

J. ⌡ Well . . . you know Russell wanted me to stay on, you know and play with the club but er one of the other things of course is that I don't have that much time these days. You know with the . . . the job's getting a bit more demanding and er . . . so,

B. What, don't you want to play with the club any more then?

J. Well of course I do, and he wants me to as well so . . . er . . . but the trouble is you know, you can't have it both ways. You got a, got a family and a . . .

B. Oh sure . . .

J. wife and family to look, to look after and . . .

B. I mean you'd you'd miss the game wouldn't you?

J. Course I would, course I would.

B. Well.

J. But er, you know, I reckon I may er I may look around elsewhere, find something, I, I . . .

Key to exercises 🔑

Unit 1   Sleeping habits

2a) 1   'I don't make the bed.'
  2   (b)
  3   Not very untidy (his side of the bed only).
  4   Try and think of something else.
  5   Only if somebody comes to the door or the telephone rings.
  6   (a); 'I'd go down and have a look around.'
  7   (a)
  8   Does not dream much.

3a) | Question no. | Question no. on questionnaire | |
|---|---|---|
| 1 | 6 | Wait to see if it happened again. |
| | | Would get up eventually. |
| 2 | 4 | I lie awake and think about things. |
| 3 | 2 | Clean my teeth; read a bit. |
| 4 | 8 | Worrying dreams. |
| 5 | 1 | No time at all. |
| 6 | 7 | Take up a lot of room. |

4a) i)   'It's a bit personal.'
  ii) 'I don't think men should be making beds, do you?'
  iii) 'I, I'm quite a quiet sleeper so they say.'
  iv) 'Oh yes. Straight out. No trouble at all.'
  v)   'No, I'd er, I'd just be angry I think. Being disturbed. Worried
       about the house, you know.'
  vi) 'I haven't had any complaints to date. No.'
       'No. I'd say I'm a very nice person to sleep with. Easy . . .'
  vii) 'I always try and remember them when I wake up if I've had a
       dream, and then it just goes . . .'

4b) i)   'Depends what sort of questions they are, ah?'
  ii) 'Well, I generally go to sleep straight away. I don't have any
       trouble getting to sleep.'
  iii) '. . . but if I read I go, I tend to go straight to sleep. I, I can
       usually read about a page and then I go straight off.'
  iv) 'Quite worrying dreams. Very worrying dreams.'
       'Well, it's rather worrying don't you think?'

84

v) 'No, I don't snore.'

vi) 'Yes. I do tend to take up more than my fair share of the bed, yes.'

vii) 'Well, I occasionally get complaints but I don't take much notice of them. What can you do?'

Unit 2 Good buys

2

Correct purchases	Alternatives purchased	Goods to return and buy
Strawberries Chicken Tomatoes Mushrooms Lettuce Wine vinegar Bread Gorgonzola	Single cream Pickling onions Pudding rice Vegetable oil	Pickling onions Herbs

4

	Goods	Excuse
i)	Single cream	I could only get single. You didn't specify.
ii)	Strawberries	I just bought a few. They were expensive.
iii)	Pickling onions	I didn't know what Spanish onions were.
iv)	Tomatoes	They aren't squashed. They are very firm.
v)	Lettuce	It has got a bit squashed. I'm sorry about that.
vi)	Vegetable oil	Olive oil is too expensive.
vii)	Rice	It will taste the same.

5 (possible answers)

i) Attitude number 2 and 3   vi) Attitude number 3 and 5
ii) Attitude number 6   vii) Attitude number 4
iii) Attitude number 2   viii) Attitude number 4
iv) Attitude number 1   ix) Attitude number 6
v) Attitude number 3 and 6   x) Attitude number 3

Unit 3 Know yourself

2 Loving – above average; selfish – average; sexy – outstanding; loyal – average; jealous – below average; secretive – below average.

5

	Woman's arguments	*Man's arguments*
Loving	'I've put up with you for the past ten years.'	
Selfish	'You don't know how to pick your programmes.'	'What about when we want to watch T.V. . . . who wins?'
Sexy		
Loyal	'I stood up for you against your brother.' 'I was just making a point.'	'What about what I heard you saying about me over the garden fence last week?'
Jealous	'I was just taking an interest in your friends the other day.'	'What about when you saw me talking to my secretary?'
Secretive	'I show you all the letters.' 'I've got the right to have a little chat now and again.'	'What about the postman?' 'What about . . . the sauna?'

6a) Loving   'Well, I wouldn't say that. I don't think.'
     Selfish   'No, no, we're filling it in about you.'
              'That's a bit one-sided.'
              'Selfish? No? I'm not selfish at all.'
              'No, I think . . .'
              'Give me an example of that!'
              'I don't think you're . . . but I don't think you're . . . either.'
     Loyal   'I wouldn't call that very loyal, would you?'
              'Well you shouldn't listen to other people's conversations.'
              'Well, I don't see why you should go washing your dirty linen in public.'
              'Rubbish, rubbish, rubbish. You shouldn't have been listening.'
     Jealous   'No.'
              'I've never been jealous.'

'I disagree, I disagree. You've got it all the wrong way
round.'
'No, no, I'm not jealous.'

Secretive 'What do you mean?'
'Huuh . . . what do you mean only one delivery?'

6b) i)   'What about this then, eh?'   Opinion
    ii)   'What about when we want to watch . . . ?'   Example
    iii) 'What about . . . Mrs er . . . Mrs Jones next door' Objection
    iv)   'What about Mrs Jones next door?'   Further
                                                         information
    v)   'What about what I heard you saying . . . ?'   Accusation
    vi)   'What about when you saw me talking . . . ?'   Accusation
    vii) 'What about all that fuss you made?'   Accusation
    viii) 'What about all that business with your
          sister . . . ?'   Accusation
    ix)   'What about when I asked you about it?'   Accusation

Unit 4   Flat hunting

1   Key to abbreviations.

b.	bathroom or	gar.	garage
	bedroom	gdn.	garden
balc.	balcony	gas c.h.	gas central
bl.	block		heating
c.h.	central heating	immac.	immaculate
conv bl.	convenience block	k & b.	kitchen and
dbl(e) b.	double bedroom		bathroom
din(er)	dining room	lge	large
eleg.	elegant	oil c.h.	oil central
exc.	excellent		heating
1st.	first	prize loc.	prize location
fitted k.	fitted kitchen	PB bl.	purpose-built
fl.	floor		block
		p.w.	per week
		recep.	reception
		sit. rm	sitting room
		spac. fam. fl.	spacious family flat
		w.	with
		w.c.	water closet

2   i)   Flat hunting for John.
    ii) Two speakers.

87

iii) Brenda – helpful, considerate, friendly.
    John   – grateful, anxious.
iv) Perhaps John and Brenda have been friends for a long time.
Brenda is allowing John to stay with her while he is flat hunting.
Brenda knows London well, but John doesn't.
Brenda has more experience of flat hunting in London than John
and is aware of the rent of flats in London.

3

	Location	Details of flats
i)	Chelsea	3 rms, k & b, ideal overseas visitors, £80, short lets available.
ii)	Bayswater	£50, 1 dbl., 1 sgl., lge recep. rm, k & b, long let.
iii)	Kensington Church St	£60.
iv)	The Angel	£37. Furnished, washing machine.
v)	Marylebone High St	
vi)	Hampstead	Ornithological views, April to October, preferably academics, c.h., £65.
vii)	Hyde Park	£100 p.w. 2 dbl. b, overlooking park.

4a)

	Discussion point	Meaning	Actual expression used
i)	Chelsea	They are asking an extortionate price for it.	'Charge you the earth for it!'
ii)	Bayswater	I really don't want to spend more than . . . I think that's expensive.	'I was thinking of spending . . .' '£50 still strikes me as pretty expensive.'
iv)	The Angel	Well, I'll think about it.	'Well, that's something to bear in mind.'
vi)	Hyde Park	Your advice is a great help, I don't think.	'Well, thanks a lot!'

4b)

	Discussion point	Meaning	Actual expression used
i)	Chelsea	Is that too expensive for you?	'Is that more than you can afford?'
ii)	Bayswater	I don't think you'll find anything cheaper. ·	'You can't do much better than that.'
vi)	Hampstead	I don't think that's what they are thinking of.	'I don't think that's what they've got in mind.'
	Conclusion	I think you should try this one in Bayswater	'I reckon you should try this Bayswater one.'

6 (possible solutions)
   i) St John's Wood.
   ii) Chelsea/St John's Wood.
   iii) Chelsea (too large but has garden).
   iv) Ken. Church St./Marylebone High St.
   v) Chelsea/St John's Wood (no garage with either).

Unit 5   Getting there

1b), 2a), 2b)

Advantages of going by ship	✓	Disadvantages of going by car	✓	Wife's objections	Advantages of going by car
Deck games	✓	Price of petrol		Be sea-sick	Freedom of road
Swimming pool	✓	Motorway tolls		Not relaxing	See countryside
Dancing		Speed traps		Old films	Visit villages,
Air-conditioned		Mending punctures	✓	Boring	churches etc.
cabins	✓	Spending money	✓	Spend a lot	Cheap drinks
Bar	✓	Searching for		Drink all the	Swim in the rivers
Films	✓	hotels		time	Need car to travel
Duty-free goods	✓	Expensive hotel		Spend holiday	across Spain.
Gambling		bills	✓	money on	
Good food/				drinks	
restaurants	✓				
Relaxation	✓				

4 i) 'Well he said they had a lovely time. Never had such a relaxing holiday.'
   ii) 'I don't believe that at all.'
   iii) 'What's relaxing about being on a boat?'
   iv) 'Such as?'
   v) 'Probably got a choice.'

vi)   'And how long's that going to take?'
vii) 'And look what it cost us . . .'
viii) 'Well, I like the idea of just paying a lump sum and there you are . . .'
ix)   'What else can you do?'
x)   'I'm sure the boat costs a fortune.'

Unit 6   Missing plans

2

	Monday	Tuesday	Wednesday	Thursday	Friday	Saturday	Sunday
1	←——In Bristol (lectures) ——→			←——Leeds (visiting mother) ——→			Return to Bristol
2	Bristol	←— Cardiff visit Sutcliffe ——→ Birmingham ←——→		Manchester visit factory	Manchester Leeds?	Lake District? Leeds?	
3	Hull warehouse	——→ Notts. (pick up parts) Birmingham ——→	Manchester (servicing)	Liverpool docks	Glasgow/ Sheffield ? football		

4   *Call 1*
i)   Anna and Bob.
ii) Bob – student/professor?
iii) Boyfriend/girlfriend – fiancé/fiancée – very good friends.

Call 2
i)   Alan Bagshot and Johnson.
ii) Bagshot – Manager of Wainwright Bros. Manchester Office.
     Johnson – Company executive or head manager of Wainwright
     Bros. Ltd.
iii) Johnson is Bagshot's superior.

Call 3
i)   Alan and Geoff.
ii) Lorry drivers for Wainwright Bros. Ltd.
iii) Good friends.

5   These are only possible solutions to an exercise about which the students may have very different opinions.

Call 1

Anna	enthusiastic	e.g. Oh, 'hello, darling.'
	disappointed	e.g. 'Oh, well, do you have to . . . ?'
		'Oh, er, early?'
	persuasive	e.g. 'You can't get back by Saturday, can you?'
		'It would be nice to see you.'
		'Do you think you could . . . ?'
		'I mean you could always sleep in . . .'
		'You don't have to get up early, do you?'
Bob	eager	e.g. 'Listen, I've worked out what I'm going to be doing for the next couple of weeks.'
	uncertain	e.g. 'Yes, well. I'll be up on Saturday, erm, but, I've got to come back to Bristol on the Sunday.'
		'Well, that, I'm not sure about yet, because . . .'

Call 2

Bagshot	placid	e.g. 'Oh yes, yes.'
		'Oh yes, that'll be to see Mr Sutcliffe, won't it?'
		'Fine.'
	respectful	e.g. 'Oh good, yes well we'll look forward to seeing you then.'
		'Well, I've got most of your details down and er I'll look forward to seeing you . . .'
Johnson	authoritative	e.g. 'It's Johnson here.'
		'I'll be sorting out a few local problems there with him.'
		'I'll be able to call into the office for erm, half an hour or so, and er, have, discuss a few points with you.'
		'There's a new designer in Leeds I want to have a chat with.'
	business–like	e.g. 'Er, just filling you in with my itinerary for the week.'
		'On Thursday, yes, and I'll clarify everything with you then.'
	self-important	e.g. 'I want to get to Birmingham on the Tuesday evening so that I rest up overnight.'

Call 3

| *Geoff* | hesitant | e.g. 'Er, I just wondered whether you could do me a favour?' |
| | | 'Well, er, I've got some er, some goods, I'd like to have taken down to er, to Hull.' |

'I wonder whether I could er, chance it, er if you could do er, a job for me?'

'But er, now this is me problem.'

'I'd er, being a keen supporter and all that, I wonder if . . .'

	anxious	e.g. 'Well, we could do, if that's all right with you.'
	blunt	e.g. 'But erm, unfortunately er, something's come up, like er, Manchester City.'
	persuasive	e.g. 'You will now, now come on, now you will now won't you?'
Alan	uncertain	e.g. 'Do, do we make the trip together to pick up the parts and go down to Birmingham on Tuesday.'
	hesitant	e.g. 'Er, to Glasgow.'
	blunt	e.g. 'Well, you want me to do you fu . . . to go to Glasgow, so you can watch City?'

'Er, ah, I, if it was United, I'd do it, but City, bloody hell, I mean.'

Unit 7 Great expectations

1b)

IDEAL QUALITIES

	What he wants	*What he does not want*
Sex	Male.	Woman.
Age	21–25	
Education	Good, two A levels, one in English.	Someone just out of university, exaggerated ideas of own importance.
Pay	Not high. Based on effectiveness. No overtime pay initially. Bonus given.	
Attitude to overtime		Someone who looks at the clock all the time.
Accent/manner	Good.	Not somebody who talks like a gutter.
Other qualities	Plenty of ambition and drive.	Married person.

3a)	A	B	C
Sex	Female	Male	Male
Age	23	18+	25 (just married)
Education	Worked abroad. Degree in English Manchester University. French/Italian.	School leaver. A level Geography. O level English.	Studying chartered accountancy. A levels – sciences and English.
Attitude to pay	Seems willing to work hard.	Not very keen on working evenings.	Uncertain.
Accent/ manner	Polite. Nice voice.	Poor accent. Manner – very direct.	Humble.
Other qualities	Ambitious, wants to go into management. Eager.	Eager to travel.	Previous experience in sales department. Wished to acquire experience.

4   'Well, I just thought it was right up my street you
know.'   enthusiasm
     'I'm not really too worried about getting a large salary
to start with.'   ambition
     'I do hope that my career as a secretary will lead me
eventually into management.'   ambition
     'Oh, can't I arrange for an interview now?'   disappointment

Unit 8   One-upmanship

2a)

Points to look for	Candidate A	Candidate B
Experience	Woolworth's supervisor 2–3 years.	Running own business, small staff – family members.
Age		
Status		Married, own house, illness in family.

Points to look for	Candidate A	Candidate B
Personal qualities		
Salary	Considers £3000 generous.	Agrees with A.

3a)

Points to look for	Candidate A	Candidate B
Experience	Assistant supervisor Woolworth's for 2 years, staff of ten. Also worked in Co-op grocery dept.	Family business – small staff of two.
Age		
Status	Doesn't mind moving.	Own house – problems in travelling.
Personal qualities – energy	Dislikes overtime.	Prepared to do overtime.
Salary	Thought offer reasonable, concerned about salary changes if moved.	Questioned travel allowance.

4c) Candidate A indulges in one-upmanship in both conversations.

Conversation 1
'Seemed to go very well indeed.'
'Managerial experience is what they're looking for isn't it?.'
'I had a big staff.'
'Don't you believe it . . . you wait until . . .'
'Travelling's going to be a bit of a problem for you, isn't it?'

Conversation 2
'I'm an assistant supervisor.'
'Staff of ten under me.'
'Before that I was with the Co-op.'
'Oh yes, I'm very experienced.'
'Oh I expect he was, yes, yes.'
'And there were my references of course.'
'I suppose you can't really bring references when you've got a family business, can you?'
'Oh, I don't know. They don't like putting transport allowances, not on top of a good wage like that you know.'

6   Idiomatic meaning (interpreted in the context of unit 8).

Meaning	*Words used on the tape*
How well did you do?	'How d'you get on?'
Quite well.	'Can't complain.'
I direct the work of . . .	'Under me.'
You're quite mistaken.	'Don't you believe it.'
She has trouble with her legs.	'Her legs are playing her up.'
A great deal/very much.	'A heck of a lot.'
I hope the person who deserves the job will get it.	'May the best man win.'
Would not be very useful.	'Wouldn't be much good.'
My flat is in the same building as my shop.	'Living on the premises.'
In addition to.	'On top of.'
Anything is possible.	'You never know.'

Unit 9   Exit 13

2a)

Alternative route	*Reasons*
A38 to 3 to 4 miles from Gloucester.	
A41★ to exit 13 to Stroud	Music festival.
Painswick	Lunch – nice pub. Nice country food, good beer, loo.
Gloucester B4073	Buy Mum's present.
A417 out of Gloucester. B4211 Snig End Tea House	Tea and gingerbreads.
A417 to M50 to Upton or B4211	If we are in a hurry.

★The man should have said A419.

3a) and b)

	A	B
Waste time eating.	5	'But it's going to take, you know, hours.'
Miss turnings and waste time.	3	'But can we, you know what it's like, we never do. We spend hours missing our turning.'
Must not drink and drive	6	'We can't drink too much though, 'cos we're driving you see.'
Get stuck in traffic.	4	'We're going to get stuck with all those damned hippies.'
Lose way on new routes.	1	'Oh I know your ways of getting to places, we always lose our way.'
Get sick through map reading.	2	'I have to read the map too and that makes me feel sick in the car.'

Unit 10   Left Out?

Solutions to exercises 2, 3, 5, 6 and 7 are merely suggestions. The students may have equally acceptable solutions.

Version 1

2 i)   Two friends of Alex.
  ii)   In their twenties/thirties.
  iii) No.
  iv)   It seems that Speaker B is feigning that she does know about the party at Alex's but has something more important to do.

3 i)   Yes.
  ii)   Alex.
  iii) Because he hasn't invited Barbara on purpose. He wants to teach her a lesson.
  iv)   No, the replies do not agree. In dialogue 2, the second speaker is not particularly concerned. In dialogue 3, the second speaker seems to think that Barbara was very upset.
  v)   The reply is dialogue 3 fits best as Barbara was upset although she feigned indifference.
  vi)   The speaker in dialogue 2 is merely answering Alex's questions. The speaker in dialogue 3 is concerned for Barbara.
  vii) The first speaker is surprised and apparently annoyed (dialogue 2). The first speaker is unrepentant and seems satisfied by the report (dialogue 3).

Version 2

4 Speaker B does not really want to go. Perhaps he would be embarrassed if he went to the party.

5 i) Yes.
   ii) Possibly Alex's new girlfriend who was Bob's (speaker B) old (ex) girlfriend.
   iii) Rather callous but curious attitude as to whether Bob cares (dialogue 2). The speaker has now reflected on the situation and perhaps feels a little guilty (dialogue 3).
   iv) According to the speaker in dialogue 2, Bob didn't seem to mind. According to the speaker in dialogue 3, Bob was very upset. Thus, the two replies don't agree.
   v) The reply in dialogue 3 fits best as Bob was upset.
   vi) The person replying does not seem very concerned, and is just reassuring the first speaker as a matter of course.
   Sid does seem to be a good friend of Bob's but tries to soften the blow by passing the blame on to Andy and his big mouth, so as not to upset the first speaker too much.
   vii) The first speaker isn't over concerned (dialogue 1). The first speaker sounds regretful at first, but does not intend to take all the blame. She accepts Sid's idea that it was Andy's fault (dialogue 2).

6a) Version 1 dialogue 1 speaker B — Offended (impression of indifference).
    Version 1 dialogue 2 speaker C — Concerned/insistent.
    Version 1 dialogue 3 speaker E — Annoyed/frustrated.
    Concerned.
    Satisfied/smug.
    Version 2 dialogue 1 speaker B — Disappointed.
    Hurt/upset.
    Version 2 dialogue 2 speaker C — Amused/frivolous.
    Version 2 dialogue 3 speaker E — Anxious/concerned.

6b) Idiomatic meanings (interpreted in the context of unit 10).

Words used on tape	Meaning
'I can't make it.'	I can't come to Alex's.
'He took it quite well.' 'He took it all in good part.'	He accepted the fact that he hadn't been invited without any fuss.
'He spilt the beans.'	He said something which he should have kept secret.
'He was dead choked.'	He was very upset.
'You could see it written all over his face.'	You could see how he felt by looking at the expression on his face.

Words used on tape	Meaning
'Just one of those things.'	It's unfortunate, but these things happen.
'He will open his big mouth.'	He is always saying things he shouldn't.
'Bloody Hell!'	
'She tried to shrug it off.'	She tried to show that it didn't bother her.
'Serves her right.'	She deserved it.

Unit 11 Football crazy, football mad

2b)

Excuses	Player's counter arguments	Real reasons	Player's reaction
i) Trouble with leg.	Ought to get exercise.	1 Pressure from supporters.	'What are you trying to say?'
ii) Distance to travel and work.	Can make up the hours.	2 He hasn't been scoring. Fouling.	'This is unjustified.' 'I play as hard as any of them.' 'I think your team is a dead loss.' 'I don't care if I ever play for you again.'
iii) Is it worth the energy? Denham – weak.	Denham has won last two matches out of three.		
iv) Try some new blood.	Should keep team as it is, experience counts.		

Manager's lies	What actually happened
i) 'I told him straight.'	The manager made excuses before 'telling him straight'.
ii) 'He was quite reasonable.'	He was very upset by the news and became angry.
iii) 'He has to work.'	John said he could make up the hours.
iv) 'He has an injury.'	The doctor said he should exercise his leg.

4a)

Reasons for not playing	Lies about telephone conversation
i) Leg takes a while to heal.	Warned manager about state of team.
ii) The team isn't up to much.	Russell wanted him to stay on.
iii) Not planning on staying.	John says he wants to continue to play with the team and that he would miss the game.
iv) Not much time with work and family.	

4b) At the beginning of the conversation, John says that the club is not doing very well and that he is thinking of leaving. At the end of the conversation however, he states that he would like to continue playing.

6a) Idiomatic meanings (interpreted in the context of unit 11).

Words used on tape	Meaning
'A bit of new blood.'	A new player.
'Experience counts.'	The team is better because they have been playing together for a long time.
'I'm only human.'	Stop evading the issue and tell me what you really mean. It's cruel to keep me guessing.
'I might as well tell you.'	I will have to tell you sooner or later.

Words used on tape	Meaning
'Let's be frank.'	I have to tell you the truth.
'If you don't mind my saying so.'	I am going to tell you exactly what I think.
'It's a dead loss.'	It's useless.
'Cards on the table.'	To tell someone all the facts.
'I told him straight.'	I told him exactly what I meant.
'Goodness knows what.'	And a lot of other things as well.
'Did he take it hard?'	Did the news upset him?
'He's getting on a bit.'	He's getting older.
'You're standing in for me.'	You're replacing me.
'About time.'	I have been waiting for this for a long time.
'The team isn't up to much.'	The team isn't very good.
'You can't have it both ways.'	One can't have all the advantages.

To the teacher

Authenticity

Analysis of genuine samples of spoken English in recent years has served to show how very different this form of the language is, not only from the written code but also from idealized notions about what spoken language 'ought' to sound like. (See D. Crystal and D. Davy, *Advanced Conversational English*, Longman 1975, and G. Brown, *Listening to Spoken English*, Longman 1977.)

The materials presented here make two assumptions:

That it is more useful to offer learners authentic-like materials than idealized, filtered samples.

That it is possible to train them in comprehension strategies to enable them to deal confidently with such materials.

No claim is made for total authenticity however. One major difficulty with genuine samples of spoken interactions is the problem of collecting them. Even if this is surmounted, such samples are often unusable owing to background noise or the sheer banality of their content. The recordings used here are 'simulated-authentic': speakers were given rough indications to work from but no scripts. What resulted was a series of spoken texts with a partially-controlled, usable content but displaying most of the linguistic features of 'ordinary conversational spoken English'.

Principles

The following principles guided us in preparing these materials.

TRAINING NOT TESTING

The materials are designed to help the student towards understanding, not to find out what he does not know. Most of the other principles are concerned with ways of doing this.

REASSURANCE

No useful purpose is served if the learner panics when faced with the materials he is to use for his learning. He needs to be reassured that he already possesses considerable knowledge and skills (often from his mother-tongue experience) which he can use to deal with the new language. He must not be hurried, but must feel that he can listen as many times as he needs and that he can share and compare his understanding with fellow students.

WHOLES TO PARTS

The materials move from more global, overall forms of understanding towards detailed attention to linguistic features of the text. This is done by a series of framing and focussing activities which help remove worry about not understanding every single word.

TASK-ORIENTED NOT QUESTION-ORIENTED

Rather than asking the learner to prove his understanding of the text by requiring him to answer questions, we have tried to provide him with tasks which use the information in the text. Apart from its motivational value, this is also somewhat closer to normal language use.

PROPS

Each unit has some form of non-aural support, in the form of pictures, plans, advertisements etc. The student is thus constantly encouraged to relate this information to the recording and his understanding is aided.

MULTI-SKILL

We believe that listening comprehension gains from being integrated with other skills. In particular we have tried to integrate it with discussion, reading and a small writing component.

GRADE TASKS NOT LANGUAGE

The fact of using non-scripted materials excludes linguistic grading. We would maintain however that, by grading the difficulty of the tasks, even lower intermediate students can use this type of material. This implies that to some degree the question of level is no longer relevant, since the same materials can be used at different levels by adjusting the difficulty of the tasks the learners are required to perform.

What the units contain

The book consists of eleven units. The overall pattern for each unit is defined as follows.

PRE-LISTENING

This is a framing activity in which students begin to familiarize themselves with the topic they will be hearing about. In most cases some kind of prop is involved – visual, verbal or a discussion. It is important not to skimp on this since it prepares students mentally for what they will hear later.

FOCUSSING ON INFORMATION

This is followed by one or more selective-listening tasks, where students are asked to search for information and record it in some way, usually by completing a grid. It is important that this be done individually to start with, but that discussion in pairs or groups should be encouraged subsequently.

FOCUSSING ON LANGUAGE

Next comes one or more tasks in which learners concentrate on what is actually said in parts of the recording and its implications for meaning.

CHECKING UP

In this section any outstanding problems can be dealt with. It is, however, most important that students try to help each other before anyone looks at the transcript. You may in fact decide that this stage is unnecessary, though it provides many students with an opportunity to integrate, restructure and fix what they may have only half-recognized. ('Aah! So that's what it was!')

RELATED ACTIVITIES

In some units there is a section involving students in role-play or some other activity related to the theme of the unit and in which they can use language and information derived from the tape.

By structuring the units in this way we have tried to be true to our principles: the topic area is framed, then first information then language are brought into focus; finally details of what was said are checked.

Some things to remember

1 The material is usable in either classroom or language
laboratory.
2 There is no need to work through the units in the order in
which they are presented nor to do all the work in any given
unit. It may be sufficient to do the information-focussing tasks.
3 Try to ensure that discussion takes place in the ways suggested.
It is important that all the modes (individual, pairs, groups,
between groups, whole class) be used.
4 Time spent in breaking down the 'I can't understand anything
if I don't understand everything' barrier will not be wasted.
Above all, students will need reassuring that they *will* be able to
do the tasks demanded of them even if they do not understand
everything.

Suggestions for teaching procedure

The following notes are offered to the teacher as a guide to the
way in which the materials in *Learning to Listen* might be
exploited.

Unit 11   Football crazy, football mad

Pre-listening

As a means of preparing the students for listening, ask them to sit
in groups of three or four and to think back in the past to a
situation (which they are willing to share with the others) where
for some reason they agreed to do something and then changed
their minds.

What was the situation?

Why did they want to get out of it?

What did they do or say in order to get out of the situation?

When they have done this, ask the students to think of a situation
(which they do not mind relating to the other members of their
group) where they have had to break some bad news to someone.

How did they break it?

What did they do/say exactly?

One of the students should act as a secretary and note down the expressions they would use to 'break the news'.

When the students are ready, ask a spokesman from each group to relate the situation in turn while another member of the group writes up their suggested expressions on the blackboard.

No doubt students will have comments to make about each other's attitudes. Allow them time to discuss any differences of opinion which exist.

Focussing on information

2a) The students have now been prepared for listening, so the tape might be introduced in the following way:
'You are now going to hear a telephone conversation between the manager of a football team and one of the players. The manager is telling the player that he will be dropped for Saturday's match; that is, he has not been chosen to play. Listen to the way in which the manager tells him this news. Do you think you would tell the player the news in the same way if you were the manager?'

Listening phase.

Now discuss with the class their reactions to the manager's approach. Encourage cross-class discussion. If the latter occurs, the teacher should try to withdraw from the conversation as much as possible.

b) Now, turn the students' attention to the grid on page 48. Explain that they are to use information from the recording to fill in the colums of the grid. Tell the students that they will only hear that part of the conversation which deals with the points in columns 1 and 2.
   e.g. 'Look at the grid on page 48. Listen to the conversation between the manager and the player again, and note down in columns 1 and 2, the excuses the manager makes for not including John in the team and also John's counter arguments. The first excuse has been filled in for you. Do not worry if you can't write all the information down. I will replay the recording for you.'

Play the tape twice if necessary before letting the students compare notes. During this comparison time, the teacher could copy the grid outline on the blackboard before asking the students to come up and fill it in. If there are any blanks left on the grid, the teacher should locate the problem area on the tape and replay it for the students. Encourage them to write up on the board whatever they hear (even a syllable or part of a word) until they gradually piece together the missing items. Follow the same procedure for columns 3 and 4 of the grid.

3   The grid completion procedure should now be quite straightforward. Introduce the second grid and telephone conversation 2. Give the students time to study the grid properly and the column headings before playing the recording. Explain that they will have to supply the information for column 2 themselves but that they may refer to the first grid if necessary.

4a) Prepare the students for conversation 3 as follows:
     'John and Bob are now in a pub, discussing the team over a beer. However, John does not want to show Bob his disappointment about not playing for the team, so he either makes excuses for not being able to play or lies about his conversation with the manager. You will now hear the conversation, but before doing so, look at the grid in which you are to enter the information.'
     Follow the technique in exercise 2 for the listening and feedback procedure. The teacher should judge whether it is necessary to put the information on the board again or whether it can be merely discussed.

  b) If the students have not noticed the inconsistency in what John says at the beginning and the end of the conversation, play the tape again. The teacher may need to lead the students to the answer by asking questions.
     e.g.   T. What do you think John's attitude to the team is?
            S. He doesn't want to play any more.
            T. (Gives quizzical look) Sure?
            (replay tape)

Focussing on language/Related activity/Group work

5   Divide the class into groups of four. Give out the problems from exercise 1 again, and ask the students to work out their roles in these situations and what they might say.

The students could then act out their role-plays. If it is possible the teacher should record them. This technique, if used sufficiently often, encourages the students to develop self and peer correction.

Focussing on language/Checking up

6   This exercise need only be selected if the teacher wishes to concentrate on intensive listening. Tell the students to look at the list of expressions on page 50. Then, one student might work the tape recorder while the others instruct him/her to stop the tape whenever they hear the particular expression to be studied. If possible the teacher should try to withdraw at this stage and leave the students to deduce the real meaning. After they have come to a consensus of opinion, they could then check their conclusions with either the teacher or the key.